KU-473-459

It's Only Natural

NO ADDED SUGAR, SALT, FATS
LOW CHOLESTEROL COOKING

Suzanne Porter

Greenhouse

Cover: Corn chowder (RD) (page 18), Wally's bread (RD) (page 80), and mixed salad (RD).

Every new recommendation by health professionals is now pointing towards a drastic lowering of fat and cholesterol. A revolution in eating habits has started in Australia, as well as the United States. Those who follow these dietary changes will assure themselves of much improved health and an active life.

Nathan Pritikin
United States dietary expert

First published in 1985 by
Greenhouse Publications Pty Ltd
385–387 Bridge Road
Richmond Victoria Australia
Reprinted 1985

© Suzanne Porter, 1985

Photography by Phil Wymant, Latrobe Studios

Typeset by ProComp Productions Pty Ltd, South Australia

Printed and bound by Impact Printing, Melbourne

ISBN 0 909104 83 2

All rights reserved. This book, or part thereof, may not be reproduced in any form without the permission of the publisher.

Distributed by Gordon & Gotch Australia Ltd
Brisbane, Sydney, Melbourne, Adelaide, Perth, Launceston

Distributed by Gordon & Gotch (NZ) Ltd
Auckland, Wellington, Christchurch, Dunedin

Foreword

The Western diet eaten by most Australians is a recipe for the early development of cardiovascular disease, obesity, diabetes, hypertension, and a host of other degenerative diseases. These rarely afflict our contemporaries who live on a more primitive diet and maintain a more active lifestyle.

Nathan Pritikin, the United States dietary expert, has demonstrated for almost thirty years that these problems are reversible by a determined change of lifestyle. The astounding benefits of his programme have been clearly validated scientifically and disseminated world-wide. Thousands of revitalized people demonstrate the dramatic benefits of this natural programme.

Some sceptics still proclaim that even twenty extra active years of life cannot compensate for the dreary dullness of the Pritikin diet. Several imaginative Pritikin recipe books have been written to disprove this claim and to show that the food not only is good but looks and tastes good. Suzanne Porter's exciting book is one of them. It is full of tested and tried Pritikin-style food from her own country kitchen and includes lots of helpful practical cooking hints on food preparation.

The whole book is set out in a clear and straightforward manner, which I believe makes it the greatest contribution to the techniques of cooking Pritikin food to date, and a safe guide to those who choose to eat their way to renewed health.

L. H. McMahon, MB, BS, FRCSI, FRCS(Edin.)
President, Pritikin Lifestyle Association

Foreword

The view has been expressed by some, that the Pritikin Diet is too restrictive and difficult to adopt as a regular part of their lifestyles, but after 9 years of unbending obedience to the Pritikin precepts since I began following them in November, 1976, I must disagree with such assertions. My experience in putting the principles into practice has always been enjoyable and satisfying and the resultant benefits have more than justified any element of challenge involved.

These days more and more people are becoming enlightened about the role of nutrition and its relationship to health. Nutritionists, Dieticians and members of the medical profession, are becoming increasingly aware that many degenerative diseases such as heart disease, high blood pressure, diabetes and indeed many forms of cancer can be prevented, and will respond favourably to dietary correction.

In my own case adherence to the Pritikin Dietary principles has brought about an almost miraculous transformation in my health. From being seriously incapacitated following a type of stroke, a heart attack and high blood pressure and suffering severe angina (chest pain) on the least exertion, to, after 18 months on the Pritikin Diet, being able to run a marathon (26 miles and 385 yards) in 3 hours, 31 minutes is an indication of the kind of response that can be obtained by this approach. Today, at 61 years of age, with normal blood pressure and off all medication through following the Pritikin Diet I have been able to complete a total of 24 marathons over 6½ years. In 1980, after 4 years on the diet at 57 years of age I was able to complete my 10th marathon in 2 hours, 58 minutes, 48 seconds.

The key to success in combating heart disease is, I believe, to reduce the amount of cholesterol in the blood to a sufficiently low level. The so called normal range for cholesterol 4–6·5 m.mols is too high and many people have cholesterol levels above that range. At 4 m.mols (total cholesterol) the 'blocking up' of our arteries (Atherosclerosis) is arrested. Below 3·8 m.mols the 'blocking up' process is slowly reversed and removal of cholesterol deposits begins. A slow process? – yes! But it works! The lower the cholesterol level, below 3·8 m.mol the faster the reversal process will be. The only effective way to lower cholesterol sufficiently for regression to occur is by dietary correction.

For everyone, the initial transition from an average Western style diet to the Pritikin diet, will certainly involve some adjustments to previously held ideas about nutrition and new dietary habits will have to be established.

Suzanne Porter, in producing this book, has made a valuable contribution to assist people in making the transition. Her comprehensive collection of recipes for enticing dishes will, I am sure, help to dispel any misconceptions about the palatability of the Pritikin diet.

Of particular importance is the distinction made by Mrs Porter, between R (Regression) and M (Maintenance) recipes. This distinction is a unique and valuable innovation and will undoubtedly help in the correct selection of dishes conforming to the appropriate version of the diet. Generally, there seems to be a lack of understanding of the Regression and Maintenance concepts within the Pritikin dietary guidelines. Even some Pritikin followers, are not aware that, to achieve the full benefits of the Pritikin diet in reversing serious degenerative disease conditions, it is essential to follow the Regression version of the diet. That simply means adding to the limitations imposed by the standard or Maintenance diet the additional limitations of (1) a maximum of 3 oz of animal protein per week, (2) a maximum of 3 pieces of fruit per day and (3) no dried fruit at all.

I am sure that recipes in this book will be inspirational, both to people commencing the Pritikin programme and to those who are already experienced in practising it. The Regression recipes marked RD may be used unreservedly whilst the Maintenance MD recipes require control over the quantities of animal protein consumed to ensure that the limits of 3½ oz per day and 1½ lb per week are not exceeded. The frequency of use of MD recipes and the quantities of each consumed will therefore require restriction, to enable conformity with the Pritikin (Maintenance) Dietary guidelines.

I strongly recommend the Pritikin Diet for people of all ages, in any state of health. I advocate the use of the recipes and adherence to this exciting dietary programme that can produce such sensationally rewarding results.

Rolet de Castella,
February, 1985

Preface

These recipes are based on some of the 'favourites' I used before I changed to the Pritikin programme, and others I created myself. It is exciting and rewarding to experiment with food, particularly if you have an appreciative family of men like mine.

The recipes are simple and easy to prepare with little fuss. They contain few herbs and spices because I prefer the subtle flavours of the main ingredients used. But it is quite in order for you to add herbs and spices if you would like their flavour.

The recipes are all suitable for the Pritikin programme. Each recipe is labelled RD (Regression Diet) or MD (Maintenance Diet). All the RD recipes are suitable for MD followers.

I wish you good luck, and most of all, good health.

Suzanne Porter

Contents

To Gordon, Mark and Scott,
whose support and encouragement never wavered

The Author wishes to thank Helene, Anita, Dot and Jill and a special thank you to my sister Wallace Thorpe, Marjorie Bowditch and Lorraine Lynas for their assistance with the photographic session.

Introduction

In 1980 I noticed a small sharp pain in my left groin if I stretched or twisted my leg. My local doctor diagnosed 'footballers groin'. After several weeks the pain became worse and I began to limp. An X-ray confirmed that I had osteo-arthritis, a degenerative disease mainly affecting the weight-bearing joints.

I was 46 years old and the future looked bleak. Lame and in constant pain, I was depressed. Having the 'wear and tear disease' meant that I could no longer play tennis, snow-ski, or cope with heavy activity. Because I was working full-time as a nursing sister in a busy hospital, and walking, lifting patients and weight-bearing are all part of a nurse's daily routine, my career was in jeopardy.

Soon after the disease was diagnosed, I read an article about the Nathan Pritikin diet and its effect on arthritis. But for me to consider changing my eating pattern was unthinkable because I loved rich, fatty, sweet food and, like most people, I was sure the food was not harmful.

Then I read *The Pritikin Program for Diet and Exercise*, became enthusiastic about it, and immediately began the Regression Diet — a simple diet aimed at avoiding cholesterol and minimizing the intake of fat, oil, and animal protein. It seemed to me that, as I had an incurable disease, giving up my Western diet was no great hardship if it would help me.

After a month I began to wonder if perseverance was worthwhile, particularly as I had no help or encouragement from friends and colleagues in the medical profession. Then I began to notice that I felt different: healthier, brighter, more energetic. I had no pain and no longer needed medication. I began to feel happy and optimistic about the future.

My last X-ray, in 1984, showed very little progression of the disease, and this slowing is, I believe, a direct result of the Pritikin programme.

I run and walk every day. I have continued with my nursing career, alternating between full and part time work. I can wear high-heeled shoes again. I am fit and active, with a blood pressure reading of 118/78. No medication is necessary.

I don't know if the programme will work for you, but if you don't try it you will never know. I do know it has worked for me.

My husband and two adult sons follow the Pritikin programme, too. How does a wife and working mother, after twenty years of cooking the conventional way, suddenly begin to prepare, cook and serve acceptable meals according to the Pritikin principles?

Nowadays it is much easier to buy the food and ingredients you need for the diet, because many manufacturers, to their credit, are supplying the needs of an every-growing health-conscious society.

We followed the Regression Diet for more than twelve months. Now we alternate the Regression Diet with the Maintenance Diet, following each for about a month. I aim to keep my cholesterol and triglyceride levels within the Pritikin recommended ranges, and have them checked every six to nine months.

I learnt to:
> cook without fat and oil
> 'dry roast' vegetables
> cook without sugar
> do without coffee and tea
> discard egg yolks
> eat unprocessed bran
> buy more vegetables
> use less meat
> make cakes, desserts, puddings, and so on, without fat, oil, sugar, egg yolks, and white flour
> find suitable food in the supermarket
> check labels for the contents of packaged and canned food.

My determination to succeed helped me to overcome difficulties. I had many cooking failures. Never again will I make a sponge-cake or a pavlova. Instead I have come to derive pleasure from experimenting with conventional recipes by substituting different ingredients. This recipe book is the result.

The food tasted bland at first, but after the first few weeks had passed I noticed that the so-called 'terrific' rich flavours of the Western diet are only those of salt or sugar.

As your taste-appreciation level alters, you begin to enjoy the subtle flavours of the food.

We would never dream of putting the wrong type of fuel into our machines or engines, yet we will continuously and thoughtlessly take the wrong food into our bodies and expect top performance!

Nathan Pritikin has drawn attention to the connection between the Western diet and degenerative diseases, such as coronary artery disease, hypertension, arteriosclerosis, adult-onset diabetes, and arthritis. His programme of diet and exercise has been fully documented and published in medical journals in many countries. Doctors recommend his programme for their patients.

The diet is high in complex carbohydrates and dietary fibre and low in animal protein, with no added salt, no added sugars, no alcohol, and no smoking. It is also low in fat and cholesterol.

Three books are essential in order to understand the Pritikin principles:

The Pritikin Program for Diet and Excerise by Nathan Pritikin with Patrick M. McGrady jun.

The Pritikin Permanent Weight-Loss Manual by Nathan Pritikin.

The Pritikin Promise: 28 Days to a Longer, Healthier Life by Nathan Pritikin.

The Diet

There are essentially two versions of the Pritikin diet: the Regression Diet and the Maintenance Diet.

- The Regression Diet is a simple diet aimed at avoiding cholesterol and minimizing the intake of fat, oil, and animal protein.
- The Maintenance Diet, on the other hand, allows a little more animal protein (about 630 grams of lean meat, fish, and poultry a week), a little extra fruit, and limited quantities of dried fruit.

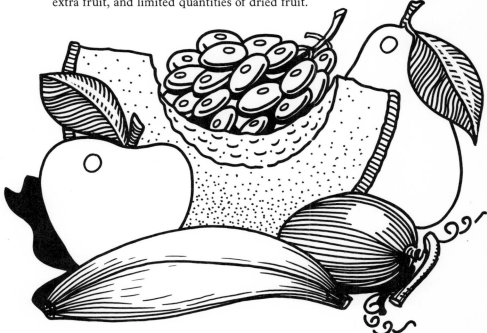

Both diets	Daily quantity
Fat or oil, unsaturated, saturated, or polyunsaturated	Nil
Salt, either sodium or potassium	Less than 4 grams
Liquid skim-milk	1 cup
Non-fat yoghurt	Little less than ¼ cup
Non-fat cheese, e.g. cottage or ricotta 1% fat by weight (maximum)	¼ cup
Potato skins, with eyes cut out (never use green ones)	Small quantities now permitted
Herbal teas (approved) and grain beverages	As desired
Herbs and spices (be careful of using black or white pepper, which can be an irritant)	As desired
Egg whites (discard yolks)	Small quantities
Nuts and seeds	Nil, except chest- nuts (raw, canned puréed, or un- sweetened spread)
Poppy seeds and sesame seeds	Sparing
Vegetables, except olives and avocados	Unlimited
Grains, except wheatgerm	Unlimited
Brown rice, unpolished	Unlimited
Stoneground wholemeal flour (to lower your sodium intake, use a sodium-free raising agent to make self-raising flour)	Unlimited (unless you aim to lose weight)

Regression Diet only

Meat, chicken or fish—must be lean and all skin removed	100 grams (3½ oz) *a week* maximum
Fruit—fresh	3 pieces *a day* (1 should be citrus)

Maintenance Diet only

Meat, chicken or fish—must be lean and all skin removed	100 grams (3½ oz) *a day* maximum
Fruit—fresh or canned	5 pieces a day (1 should be citrus)

Weight Control

If you are overweight, your weight-bearing joints have an increased amount of work to do, especially the hip joints. Knees and hips are targets for osteo-arthritis and the disease is difficult to control in these areas. It is absolutely essential that you maintain your weight within the limits recommended for your build and height. This can be achieved with the Pritikin programme.

I have weighed between 52 and 53 kilograms since beginning the programme in 1981. My weight variation depends on the amount of grains and vegetables I have eaten each week.

Over the past four years I have found that I can literally eat like a horse of the acceptable foods and not gain any weight. Friends and relatives are astounded at the amounts of food that I eat, particularly when they are 'dieting' to lose weight on the Western diet and almost starving themselves. It is fun trying to convince them that the Pritikin diet freely permits the carbohydrates they were trying to avoid.

If the programme helps you to not only lose weight but to have increased mobility without pain, giving up the foods that are causing your discomfort should not be a hardship.

There are excellent weight-loss and weight-control guides and information in *The Pritikin Permanent Weight-Loss Manual*.

Helpful hints

- Eat at least six to eight small meals a day.
- Soup is filling and weight reducing.
- Have salad vegetables on hand: they may be eaten raw, cooked or lightly steamed. Eat them at any time during the day.
- Use fresh fruit as a sweetener, or use Date Purée (page 83).
- Bread may be eaten if it does not contain salt, sugar, animal fat, or vegetable oils.
- Wherever possible, grow your own vegetables, or buy them organically grown.
- Ricotta 1% fat cheese is available commercially from some supermarkets and health food stores in Melbourne. One per cent fat ricotta is the maximum allowed for either of the diets. If it is unavailable, you can make your own from skim milk, or use my recipe.
- Use garlic, herbs, spices, lemon, and vinegar to flavour your cooking.
- To ensure that you get the most vitamins from food:
  Wash vegetables, but do not soak them because they lose vitamins B and C.
  If possible, cut fruit and vegetables just prior to eating them. They lose vitamins when left standing.
  Steam vegetables whenever possible, or eat them raw, or cook them in a minimum of water.
  If you use frozen vegetables, don't thaw them but put them straight into the pot.
  Don't use bicarbonate of soda (baking soda) when cooking vegetables. It destroys thiamin (vitamin B_1) and vitamin C. It also increases your sodium (salt) intake.
- Added salt is not permitted on either of the diets, but sodium (salt) is found in abundant quantities in leafy green vegetables and raw fruits. Dried fruits are rich in sodium. Celery, parsley, carrots, and brown rice are some other sources of sodium. Adding salt is unnecessary as there is adequate for the body's use in the foods we eat.
- Strawberries raise the uric acid level which aggravates arthritis and gout. Use them in moderation.

Using the recipes

Measuring the ingredients

To help readers who may have difficulty preparing food and changing from the Western diet, I have made most quantities as simple as possible by using cup and spoon measurements. Those people who have a busy daily schedule and do not have the time to use weighing methods will also find this helpful.

All measurements are level.

Graduated spoons (metric)

¼ teaspoon
½ teaspoon
1 teaspoon   Use either for dry or for liquid ingredients
1 tablespoon

Graduated measuring cups (metric)

¼ cup
⅓ cup   Use either for dry or for liquid ingredients
½ cup
1 cup

Oven temperatures	C	F
Very slow	120°	250°
Slow	140°	300°
Moderate	180°	375°
Hot	210°	400°
Very hot	230°	450°
Extremely hot	240°	500°

Cooking utensils

Some kitchen utensils are essential, although it isn't necessary to buy them all at once.

Electric blender or food processor
Non-stick frying-pan
Steamers and double saucepan
Glass or plastic mixing bowls
Non-stick cake tins and trays*
Plastic slide for non-stick pan
Grater
Tongs
Potato-masher
Vegetable crisper
Aluminium foil
Oven bags

----

* Tins and trays can be lined with foil if you haven't non-stick ones. After a cake is cooked, put it straight from the oven into an airtight tin for about twenty minutes. Then the foil can be removed easily.

Abbreviations

cm	centimetre
g	gram
MD	Maintenance Diet
RD	Regression Diet
ml	millilitre
SR	self-raising
SG	stone ground

Soups

A bowl or mug of filling, nourishing soup may be eaten once every day, or more often if you feel hungry. Always keep soup in the refrigerator as a standby. Unlimited quantities of soup may be eaten by followers of either of the diets.

Most of these recipes can be made while you are preparing the evening meal. When cooking the vegetables, remember to save the water to use as stock.

Vegetable stock can be made by cooking together any vegetables and saving the water.

To make vegetable soup, cook a combination of your favourites and add grains to give thickness and variety.

Meat, fish or chicken stock must be free of all fat. It is helpful to freeze the stock, and when it is needed the fat on the surface can be scraped off, or run off with boiling water. Only then can the stock be used.

Stock is not always necessary for making soups. I substitute water with great success.

Each recipe makes two to four serves.

Cauliflower soup

¼ fresh cauliflower

1 small onion, chopped

1 small potato, chopped

2 cups stock, fat free (or water)

1 tablespoon cornflour

¼ cup skim-milk powder

Prepare all the ingredients, except the skim milk and cornflour, and place in a saucepan. Bring to the boil and simmer for 25 minutes.

With a potato-masher, gently mash the ingredients to a chunky consistency. To thicken, add the cornflour and skim milk mixed to a paste with water.

Variations
1. Prepare as above, but blend in a blender. Thicken as above. Garnish with parsley.
2. For extra flavour, add a dash of garlic powder, nutmeg and paprika.
3. Add to the soup ½ cup grated 1% fat (maximum) skim-milk cheese 5 minutes before serving.

Corn chowder

2 cups fresh corn off the cob

2 medium-sized potatoes, diced

1 medium-sized onion, diced

3 cups chicken stock, fat free

½ cup skim-milk powder

Place all the ingredients in a saucepan and gently simmer until they are cooked and the soup is thick.

Before serving, add the skim milk (mixed with a little water).

Cream of carrot soup

2 medium-sized carrots, chopped

1 medium-sized onion, chopped

4 cups chicken stock, fat free

Pinch garlic powder

Pinch nutmeg

¼ cup skim-milk powder

1 tablespoon cornflour

1 tablespoon parsley, chopped

Place all the ingredients except the skim-milk powder, cornflour and parsley into a saucepan. Bring to the boil and simmer for about 30 minutes. Cool, and place into a blender or through a sieve.

Return the soup to the saucepan; add the milk and cornflour mixed with a little water.

Stir in the parsley just before serving.

Cucumber soup

1 large cucumber, peeled and
  chopped
1 onion, peeled and chopped
3 cups chicken stock, fat free
Small piece cucumber peel for
  flavour

Seasoning to taste
¼ cup skim-milk powder
Extra cucumber slices to garnish

Toss the prepared vegetables, with a little of the stock, in a non-stick frying pan. Do not brown.

Transfer to a saucepan of stock and add the peel and seasoning. Simmer the soup for 20 minutes.

Blend it in an electric blender, and add the skim milk mixed to a paste with water.

Chill it. Serve topped with sliced cucumber.

Easy vegetable soup

1 medium-sized potato, chopped
1 small carrot, sliced
1 small onion, sliced and chopped
1 cup cauliflower
1 zucchini, chopped, skin left on
1 stalk celery, finely chopped
½ cup diced pumpkin

½ cup corn off the cob
½ cup green peas
garlic for flavour
3 cups cold water, or more
1 tablespoon tomato paste or
  granules, salt free (optional)

Prepare and place all the ingredients in a saucepan, and simmer them gently until tender and reasonably thick. Add the garlic, and extra water if necessary.

If you like, lightly mash the vegetables with a potato-masher.

For extra flavour add the tomato paste or granules.

Variation
This soup may be made into Cream of Vegetable soup by adding ⅓ cup non-fat skim-milk powder (mixed with water). It may also be thickened with a little cornflour.

MD ## Lobster chowder

1 cup lobster pieces, cooked and
  fat free
1 cup corn off the cob
1 medium-sized onion, diced
3 cups chicken stock, fat-free

1 tomato, diced
1/2 cup skim-milk powder
1/4 teaspoon garlic powder
Pinch each nutmeg and paprika

Place all the ingredients into a saucepan, except the skim milk. Gently simmer until thick and tender. Add the skim milk (with a little water) just before serving.

RD ## Potato and green pea soup

2 large potatoes, peeled and diced
1 large onion, peeled and diced
4 cups chicken or vegetable stock,
  (fat free)

1³/₄ cups green peas
Bouquet garni
Sprig of mint
1/2 cup skim-milk powder

Prepare the potatoes and onion and toss them in a non-stick frying pan with a little stock; do not brown them. Add the remaining stock, bring this to the boil, and simmer for 15 minutes. Add the peas, bouquet garni, and mint, and cook for a further 30 minutes. Remove the bouquet garni. Blend the soup in a blender. Add the skim-milk powder mixed with a little water. Serve hot.

MD ## Salmon chowder

220 gm can pink or red salmon
2 medium-sized potatoes, diced
1 medium-sized onion, diced

3 cups fish or chicken stock, fat free
1/4 cup skim-milk powder

Flake the fish, remove the skin and bones, and rinse the fish under the tap.
  Cook the potato and onion in the stock until thick and tender. Add the prepared salmon, and simmer for 10 to 15 minutes.
  Add the skim milk powder, mixed with water, just before serving.

Tomato soup

6 ripe, medium-sized tomatoes,
 peeled
2 medium-sized onions, chopped
2 cups vegetable stock, fat free

1 clove garlic, crushed
1 tablespoon tomato paste, salt free
¼ cup skim-milk powder (optional)
Cornflour to thicken

Gently simmer all the ingredients, except the skim milk powder and cornflour. Remove, and purée in a blender. Add the skim-milk powder and tomato paste, and thicken with the cornflour mixed with some water.

Tomato basil soup

1 can tomato purée, salt free if
 possible
1 medium-sized onion, thinly sliced
¼ teaspoon basil, dried

1 teaspoon Date Purée (optional),
 page 83
1 cup chicken stock, fat free

Sauté the onion in a small amount of the stock. Add all other ingredients, cover and gently simmer until slightly thickened for about 20 minutes.
   Serve with toasted Pritikin bread and garnish with basil leaves.

Vegetable and rice soup

2 carrots, sliced
2 sticks celery, chopped
2 medium-sized onions, chopped
1 zucchini, chopped
1 cup mushrooms, chopped

4 cups stock, fat free
4 cups water
½ cup brown rice
1 tablespoon tomato paste, salt free
½ cup skim-milk powder

Prepare all the vegetables. Place all the ingredients, except the skim-milk powder, into a saucepan and bring to the boil. Simmer gently until the rice is cooked and the soup is thick.

Add the skim milk mixed with water just before serving.

Salads

Except for olives and avocados, there is no limit to the types of fruit and vegetables that can be combined to make delicious salads, providing that you stay within the guidelines of the Pritikin diets.

The recipes include some combinations that I serve to my family and guests. Our enjoyment of these tempting salads is equal to my pleasure in creating them, or in adapting Western-style salads to suit the diets. Try mine, or invent or adapt some of your own.

MD # Ambrosia salad

1 cup mandarin segments
1 medium-sized red apple,
  chopped
2 medium-sized bananas, sliced
1/2 cup pitted dates, chopped

2 tablespoons non-fat yoghurt and
  1% fat (maximum) ricotta, mixed
  together
Lettuce cups

Prepare the fruit and toss it in the yoghurt and ricotta mixture. Spoon it into the lettuce cups.
  Serves 4.

RD # American side salad

1 cup green beans, cooked and
  chopped
1 cup corn, cooked and removed
  from cob
1 red pepper, finely diced

1/2 cup raw mushrooms, sliced
1 firm ripe tomato, sliced
1/2 cup French Dressing
  (page 85)
Onion rings

Toss all the ingredients in French Dressing, pour into a glass dish and garnish with the onion rings.
  Serves 4.

RD # Carrot salad (1)

1 cup carrot, freshly grated
1 cup unsweetened pineapple pieces,
  fresh or canned

Mix together the carrots and pineapple and serve as a side dish.

MD # Carrot salad (2)

2 cups carrot, freshly grated
1/4 cup natural sultanas

1/4 cup Mayonnaise (page 87)

Mix together all the ingredients and place in glass dish.
  Serves 1–2.

Carrot surprise

1 cup carrot, raw, grated
½ cup salad onion, chopped
½ cup celery, chopped

Grated orange peel
1 orange, peeled and wedged
Lettuce leaves

Prepare and toss all ingredients and place into a wooden bowl lined with lettuce leaves.
Serves 4.

Chicken peach salad

1 cup chicken pieces, cooked, skin
  and all fat removed, and diced
1 canned peach, unsweetened and
  sliced
Medium-sized crisp lettuce leaves
Celery

1 fresh pear, with skin on
6 dried dates, halved and pitted
Watercress
⅓–½ cup Mayonnaise (page 87)
Lemon to garnish

Cut the celery in 6 cm lengths. Split one end of each piece, and dip it into iced water to curl it.
  Slice the pear lengthwise.
  Pit the dates and cut them into rings.
  Line a wooden bowl with the lettuce and place the vegetables and chicken in an attractive arrangement. Top with the prepared mayonnaise and the fruit.
  Serves 1–2.

Coleslaw cabbage

2 cups cabbage, shredded
½ cup celery, chopped
½ cup carrot, grated
½ cup fresh pineapple, finely cut

½ cup green or red pepper, chopped
  (optional)
¼ cup red cabbage, shredded
½ cup Mayonnaise (page 87)

Prepare all the ingredients and combine them. Fold the mayonnaise into the mixture.
  Serves 4.

RD

Hot potato salad

4 medium-sized potatoes
2 celery stalks, chopped
1 Mignonette lettuce

1 medium-sized salad onion, sliced
 in rings

Lemon dressing
3 tablespoons lemon juice
3 tablespoons unsweetened apple
 juice

3 tablespoons white vinegar
1 clove crushed garlic
2 tablespoons parsley, chopped

Cook the potatoes in their jackets, drain, and cut into medium-sized pieces. Line salad bowl with the outside leaves of lettuce, washed, and drained.

Tear up the remaining lettuce leaves and place in the salad bowl. Add the hot potatoes, celery and onion. Pour the lemon dressing over. Serve at once.

To make the lemon dressing, combine all the ingredients and pour them over the prepared salad.

Serves 4–6.

RD

Mushroom slaw

1 cup raw mushrooms, sliced
1 green apple, unskinned and cut
 into chunks
1 red apple, unskinned and cut into
 chunks

1 cup celery, cut up
½ cup Mayonnaise (page 87)

Prepare all the ingredients and toss them in the mayonnaise.

Serves 4.

RD

Pasta slaw

1 cup cabbage, shredded
1 green pepper, chopped
1 carrot, grated
1 cup wholemeal pasta noodles,
 cooked

½ cup Mayonnaise (page 87)
A few cabbage leaves

Combine all the ingredients and toss them lightly. Pour them into a wooden bowl lined with the cabbage leaves.

Serves 4.

Pear and chicken salad

2 pear halves, fresh, or unsweetened canned	1 tablespoon Date Purée (page 83)
	1 tablespoon lemon juice
1 cup fat free chicken or turkey (white meat only), cooked and cubed	½ cup celery, sliced
	Lettuce leaves
	Two strawberries (optional)
¼ cup yoghurt, fat-free	

Combine the yoghurt, Date Purée and lemon juice, and gently fold in the celery and meat. Spoon into the two lettuce leaves and serve on two plates. Add pear half to each plate. Garnish each with a fresh strawberry (optional).

Serves 2.

Pineapple salad

2 pineapple rings, fresh, or unsweetened canned	4 slices of cucumber
	1 scoop cottage cheese, fat-free
1 lettuce cup	½ red apple, dipped in lemon juice
1 orange, peeled and sliced	

Arrange the lettuce cup on a plate, then arrange the pineapple, orange slices and cucumber. Place scoop of cottage cheese in the centre and garnish with the apple slices dipped in lemon juice.

Serves 1.

Rice salad

2 cups brown rice, cooked	½ cup French Dressing
½ cup green peas, cooked and cold	(page 85) (optional)
½ cup corn, cooked and cold	

Combine all the ingredients and fold in the French Dressing.
   To make a large quantity, add more of the ingredients.

RD

Tasty beetroot

2 beetroot, medium size
½ cup vinegar
¼ cup fresh orange juice
Glass jar with lid

Cook, cool, peel and slice beetroot into glass jar. Pour over vinegar and juice mixed together. Replace lid. Store in refrigerator.

Variation
Substitute orange juice for same quantities of unsweetened pineapple juice of unsweetened apple juice.

RD

Tomato salad

2 medium-sized tomatoes, sliced
½ cucumber, skin removed, scored,
  and cut into rings

1 small salad onion, cut into rings
½ cup vinegar

Prepare the ingredients. Place them in a glass dish, and pour the vinegar over them about 30 minutes before serving.

RD

Watermelon delight

2 cups watermelon, cut into chunks,
  pips removed
1 cup orange slices

½ cup salad onion rings
½ cup Mayonnaise (page 87)
(optional)

This salad is delightful, either with or without the mayonnaise, with yoghurt.

Vegetable dishes

Fresh vegetables served in attractive combinations and cooked to perfection, with piquant herbs and spices if you like, are an important part of your diet. The fresher the vegetables are, the better.

Except for olives and avocados, all vegetable combinations are suitable for both diets, providing that no oil, fat, salt, or sugar are added. Unlimited quantities may be eaten.

It is important not to overcook vegetables. They are delicious crisp-cooked. Steamed, they retain their flavour, vitamins, and minerals.

There is no need to eat potatoes sparingly because they are not fattening if eaten without oils and fats.

When cooking, try to remember to save the vegetable water to use as stock. Save the tops of celery, too, to use in soups.

Asparagus and mushrooms

RD

6 stalks
*Fresh asparagus, cut diagonally
  in short pieces*
1 small onion, minced

½ cup button mushrooms, sliced
½ cup liquid skim milk
1 teaspoon cornflour

Add all the ingredients, except the cornflour, and cook for 10 minutes, gently tossing them. Thicken with the cornflour mixed to a paste with water. Serve hot.
  Serves 2–3.

Baked potatoes

RD

*4 medium-sized potatoes, preferably
  old ones as they bake better than new*

Scrub and dry potatoes. Prick them with a fork. Place them on a baking tray and bake in moderately hot oven for about 1 hour.

Suggested fillings

Corn and cheese: Cut the tops off the baked potatoes, remove the pulp and mash it with liquid skim milk and a small quantity of 1% fat (maximum) grated cheese. Top with cooked corn. Re-heat in the oven and serve.

Tomato and mushroom: Method as above. Omit the corn and cheese and top with sliced tomato and mushrooms. Re-heat in the oven and bake a further 10 to 15 minutes. Serve hot.

Baked in foil

Baked potatoes may be served soft by wrapping each in foil before baking in a moderately hot oven for about an hour.

Broccoli au gratin

RD

2 stalks fresh green broccoli
½ cup stock, fat free (or water)
1 cup White Sauce (page 92)

*Grated skim-milk cheese, 1% fat
  (maximum) – optional*

Sauté the broccoli in the liquid for 5 to 10 minutes. Place in a casserole dish. Pour the White Sauce over, and top with the grated cheese. Brown under the griller. Serve at once.
  Serves 2.

Carrots

RD

Glazed

RD

Cut up carrots into rings. Cook for 5 minutes in minimum water. Drain.
Add 1 tablespoon of Date Purée if liked (page 83).

Carrot rings

MD

As above. Add a dash of garlic powder and twelve sultanas. Remove the
sultanas just before eating.

Carrot with Apricot Purée

RD

Gently simmer carrot rings for 5 minutes in a small quantity of
unsweetened apricot purée.

Chinese-style vegetables

RD

3 cups cabbage, finely shredded
2 medium-sized celery stalks, cut
  diagonal slices
1 medium-sized green pepper
  (optional)
3/4 cup onion, chopped

Pinch garlic powder
Pinch nutmeg
4 tablespoons stock, fat free (or
  water)
1/2 cup bean shoots

Place all the ingredients in a non-stick frying-pan. Toss them contantly
for about 5 minutes. Serve at once.
   Serves 2–4.

Creamed celery

RD

5 stalks celery, cleaned and chopped
4 tablespoons water (or fat free
  stock)

1 cup White Sauce (page 92)
Garlic (optional)

Lightly toss the celery in the stock (or water) in a non-stick pan for 3 to 4
minutes, with the lid on. Add the White Sauce. Serve at once.
   Serves 1–2.

RD

Easy cabbage

4 cups cabbage, shredded
½ cup stock, fat free (or water)

Toss the ingredients in liquid in a non-stick frying pan for 5 to 10 minutes. Serve at once.
  Serves 4.

RD

Easy roast potatoes

Required number of potatoes for
  Virginia Roast (page 56)

Peel and prepare the potatoes.
  Place the pieces in a non-stick frying pan and replace the lid. Have the hot plate at medium heat. Turn the potatoes every 10 minutes with a plastic slide, and brown them on all sides. Continue until the potatoes are cooked and resemble conventional roasted potatoes.

RD

Fried rice

2 cups cooked brown rice
2 egg whites (discard yolks)
¼ cup carrot grated
¼ cup celery, sliced

¼ cup cooked peas
¼ cup cooked corn off the cob
1 teaspoon low-salt soy sauce
¼ cup onion, or chives, chopped

Cook the egg white in a non-stick frying pan. Cut it up. Add the rest of the ingredients, gently tossing them until hot and cooked. Serve hot.
  Serves 4.

Pizza supreme (RD) (page 41) using Wholemeal pastry (page 110) with (from top left) Tasty beetroot (RD) (page 28), Quick tasty tomato sauce (MD) (page 89) and Sautéed apples, onions and sultanas (MD) (page 35).

Green beans and mushrooms RD

2 cups cooked beans, chopped
½ cup sautéed mushrooms, finely
  chopped

Lightly toss together the beans and mushrooms. Serve at once.
  Serves 2.

Green peas with potato in cream sauce RD

2 medium-sized potatoes, peeled,
  diced, and cooked
1 cup freshly cooked peas

Small quantity White Sauce (page
  92) — for stock use water from
  vegetables

Combine cooked potatoes and peas. Add the White Sauce and serve.
  Serves 3.

Hash browns RD

4 medium-sized potatoes, grated
2 tablespoons onion, finely chopped

1 egg white (discard yolk)

Squeeze the excess liquid out of the grated potatoes, add the chopped onion and egg white. Place this mixture into a non-stick frying pan, and brown. With a slide separate the mixture into portions. Brown each side and serve hot.
  Serves 4.

Curried chicken with apricots (MD) (page 51), served with Steamed broccoli (RD), Carrot surprise (RD) (page 25) and Carbonated apple juice, unsweetened (MD).

33

RD
Lemon chive potatoes

10 small new potatoes
½ teaspoon lemon peel, grated
2 teaspoons snipped chives

Pinch garlic powder
Pinch nutmeg, grated
Small quantity potato water

Wash the potatoes. Boil them and cook until tender. Drain, and remove the skins. Heat the remaining ingredients and pour them over the potatoes. Serve at once.
Serves 4–5.

RD
Potatoes in yoghurt

Ingredients as for Lemon Chive
  Potatoes, but omit lemon
  and potato water

½ cup yoghurt, fat and sugar free

Prepare as for Lemon Chive Potatoes, but leave skins on the potatoes and halve them. Pour the mixture over the cut potatoes with yoghurt. Serve hot or cold.
Serves 4–5.

RD
Potato vegetable pie

2 cups vegetable combination of
  your choice, cooked in minimum of
  water
2 tablespoons skim-milk powder
1 tablespoon cornflour

Some pre-cooked mashed potato for
  topping
Grated skim-milk cheese, 1% fat
  (maximum)– optional

Place the ingredients in a saucepan and gently simmer them for 5 to 10 minutes. Thicken with the skim milk and cornflour mixed to a paste with water. Pour into a casserole or pie dish.
  Spread the potato on top with the grated cheese. Bake in the oven and serve hot.
Serves 2–3.

Variation
For different flavour, add 1 tablespoon tomato paste, salt free.

Sautéed apples, onions and raisins or sultanas

MD

4 red apples, unpeeled and cored, cut into eighths
8 medium white onions peeled and quartered

⅓ cup natural sultanas or raisins
¼ cup chicken stock, fat free

Sauté the apples and onions with the chicken stock in a non-stick frying pan, tossing them very gently. Cook, covered, for 5 minutes only.
  Add the sultanas or raisins, slowly cook, uncovered, until the apples and onions are tender. Serve as an entrée, or with a meat dish.
  Serves 4.

As above, but omit the dried fruit.

RD

Stuffed butternut pumpkin

RD

1 medium-sized butternut pumpkin
1 large onion, chopped
1 clove garlic

1 cup cooked brown rice
4 tomatoes, peeled and chopped
Dash of basil

Sauté the onion in a little water in a non-stick frying pan. Add the garlic, rice and tomatoes.
  Cut the pumpkin in half lengthwise and remove the seeds. Stuff the halves with the mixture. Bake in a moderate oven for about 30 minutes, or until the pumpkin is cooked.

RD ## Sue's vegetable combo

1 medium-sized onion, in rings
1 medium-sized carrot, sliced in
  discs
5 stalks fresh asparagus, cut up
¼ cauliflower, cut up
1 potato, chopped and peeled
1 cup corn off the cob

1 celery stalk, sliced
Grated skim-milk cheese, 1% fat
  (maximum) – optional
2 tablespoons cornflour
¼ cup skim-milk powder
¼ teaspoon paprika
1 cup stock, fat free (or water)

Prepare all the vegetables and place them in a saucepan with the cup of
liquid. Bring to the boil and simmer for 10 minutes only. Remove the
saucepan from the heat. (Save the vegetable water for later use.) Thicken
the cornflour with a little water, mix into it the skim-milk powder and
paprika, and stir this mixture into the vegetables. Pour into the casserole
dish. Top with grated cheese if you like, and brown in the oven. Serve hot.
  Serves 3–4.

Variation
1. Use your own combination of favourite vegetables. Prepare and serve
   in same manner.
2. For extra flavour, add clove of garlic or a dash of nutmeg.

RD ## Tomato and onion casserole

4 ripe tomatoes, sliced
1 medium-sized onion, in rings
2 tablespoons stock, fat free (or
  water)

1 slice Pritikin bread

Prepare the vegetables and arrange them in a casserole dish. Add the stock
(or water).
  Cut the bread into four pieces and arrange them on top of the tomatoes.
Bake in a moderate oven until cooked. This may be served with a roast.
  Serves 4.

Main dishes with vegetables

Any of these tasty dishes can be eaten in large quantities by followers of either of the diets. Vegetables are the main ingredients.

Suitable for lunches or dinners, the recipes include pies, pancakes, pasta, casseroles, quiche, patties . . . and they are enhanced by the popular flavours of yoghurt, tomato paste, cheese, kidney beans, mushrooms, garlic, and many others.

RD ## Corn patties

4 medium-sized potatoes, cooked
  and dry-mashed
1 small onion, diced
1 cup corn off the cob, cooked
½ cup peas, cooked

Unprocessed bran for covering
  patties
Pinch each sage, basil and oregano
Pinch cayenne pepper

Mix the potatoes, onion, corn, peas and herbs together. Make large spoonfuls into round flat patties. Coat each in the bran. Brown both sides in a non-stick frying pan.

Serve with hot vegetables, or your favourite salad.

Makes 6–7.

RD # Individual wholemeal vegetable pies

Enough Savoury Wholemeal Pastry
  (page 109) to make 4 individual
  vegetable pies
4 cups mixed vegetables of your
  choice, cooked, thickened and
  cooled

Pinch garlic powder
Low-fat yoghurt, sugar free
Small amount grated cheese, 1% fat
  (maximum) or fat free

Make the pastry. Cook the vegetables with the garlic powder. Thicken them. Cool.

Line four non-stick pie tins with the rolled-out pastry. Fill with the thickened vegetables. Top each with a pastry lid.

Brush lightly with the yoghurt, and make a small hole in the top of each. Sprinkle with the cheese.

Bake in a moderate oven until brown.

Serves 4.

Variation

These may be made as very small party pies, using the above method.

Lasagne

6 ripe tomatoes, cut up
2 medium-sized onions, chopped
1 clove of garlic, crushed
Pinch each nutmeg, basil, oregano
1 cup tomato paste, low salt or
  salt free

1 tablespoon cornflour
1 cup 1% fat (maximum) cheese,
  grated
2 cups non-fat yoghurt, sugar free
2 large wholemeal pita breads

Cook the tomatoes, onions, garlic, herbs and spices in a non-stick frying pan until they are soft. Add the tomato paste. Thicken with the cornflour mixed with a little water.

Pour about half of the mixture into an ovenproof dish. Sprinkle with a little of the cheese and spread with the yoghurt. Place on top one pita bread cut to the required size. Repeat as before, ending with pita bread on top. Finally, lightly spread with the remainder of the mixture, a little yoghurt, and top with the rest of the cheese.

Bake in a moderate oven.

Serves 4–6.

Pasties

1 large potato, peeled and chopped
1 medium-sized onion, chopped
½ cup celery, chopped
½ cup mushrooms, chopped
1 medium-sized carrot, grated
½ cup green beans, chopped
1 tablespoon stock, fat free (or water)

1 tablespoon soy sauce, low salt
Pinch nutmeg
Pinch garlic powder
Cornflour
Quantity of Wholemeal Pastry (page 110)
Small quantity low-fat yoghurt, sugar free

Prepare all the vegetables and gently simmer them in a non-stick frying pan with the stock or water for 10 minutes only. Do not brown.

Add the soy sauce, nutmeg, and garlic powder. Thicken with the cornflour mixed with water. Allow to cool.

Prepare the pastry. Roll it out thinly and cut into pasty-sized circles. Place spoonfuls of filling on to the pastry and fold over, pinching together the open sides.

Lightly brush the tops with the yoghurt and put three tiny slits on the top of each. Bake in a moderate oven until the pasties are lightly browned.

Variation

You can use any combination of your favourite vegetables.

Pizza

4 ripe tomatoes, peeled
1 medium-sized onion, chopped
1 clove garlic
200 g tomato paste, salt free
Pinch each basil and oregano
½ cup 1% fat (maximum) cheese,
  grated

¾ cup drained pineapple pieces,
  fresh or unsweetened
1 large wholemeal pita bread,
  (or Wholemeal Pastry, page 110)

Preheat the oven to moderate.

Simmer the tomatoes, onion and garlic in a non-stick frying pan until they are soft. Add the herbs and tomato paste. Spread on to the pita bread or pastry on a medium-sized pizza tray.

Top with grated cheese and arrange pineapple pieces. Bake for 15 minutes.

Variations

Add 1 cup sliced mushrooms, or ¼ cup each green and red peppers, or ½ cup cooked chopped egg white, or make up a combination of all of these above to make a Pizza Supreme.

Potato quiche

Enough mashed potato to line a
  medium-sized quiche dish
1 cup mixed vegetables, diced and
  cooked
½ onion, chopped
½ cup cooked corn
¼ cup cooked peas

¼ cup cooked green beans
Pinch each garlic powder,
  cayenne pepper, basil, and sage
1½ cups ricotta cheese, non-fat or
  1% fat (maximum)
3 egg whites (discard yolks)

Line a quiche dish with the mashed potato. Mix all the vegetables and herbs and spices together with the ricotta and egg whites. Spread over the potato base. Bake in a moderate oven for 35 to 40 minutes until the filling has set.

Serves 3–4.

RD ## Red kidney beans

1½ cups red kidney beans,
  washed and dried
6 cups water

Boil the beans for 2 minutes. Cover them and let stand for 1 hour, then cook until tender. Drain and cool.
  Use in casseroles, soups, or main dishes of your choice.

RD ## Silver beet pie

2 cups silver beet, cooked and
  shredded
4 spring onions
¼ cup ricotta cheese, 1% fat
  (maximum), or non-fat
½ cup cottage cheese, non-fat

2 egg whites (yolks discarded)
Small quantity Wholemeal
  Pastry (page 110)
½ cup grated cheese, 1% fat
  (maximum)

Sauté onions in a non-stick frying pan with a little water. Add the silver beet. Turn off the heat. Mix the ricotta and cottage cheese in a blender with the egg whites. Fold this into the vegetable mixture, and then turn it into a pastry-lined ovenproof pie dish.
  Top with grated cheese. Bake in a moderate oven for ¾ hour.
  Serves 2–4.

RD ## Spaghetti

3 cups Pizza Topping (page 41)
Small quantity of cooked
  wholemeal spaghetti

½ cup grated cheese, 1% fat
  (maximum)

Prepare the pizza topping and pour it over the cooked spaghetti. Top with grated cheese. Serve hot.
  Serves 2–4.

Vegetable bean flan

4 zucchini, chopped very finely
1 medium-sized onion, chopped
1 clove garlic, crushed
1 tablespoon stock, fat free (or
  water)
1 cup red kidney beans, cooked

1 tablespoon parsley, chopped
1/3 cup liquid skim milk
2 egg whites (discard yolks)
Pinch nutmeg
1 baked Wholemeal Pastry flan
  (page 110)

Bake the pastry flan.

Sauté the chopped zucchini, onion, and crushed garlic in the stock or water until soft. Cool. Add the beans, parsley, skim milk, beaten egg white, and nutmeg. Pour into the flan. Sprinkle with the grated cheese. Bake in a moderate oven for 30 to 35 minutes.

Serves 4–6.

Vegetable casserole

2 medium-sized potatoes,
  quartered
1 medium-sized onion, sliced
1 cup mushrooms, sliced
1 medium-sized carrot, sliced in
  chunks
1/2 cup corn, cooked
1/2 cup peas, cooked
1/2 cup celery, sliced in chunks

2 cups stock (chicken if possible),
  low fat
Pinch garlic powder
Pinch nutmeg
1 tablespoon cornflour
1 tablespoon skim-milk powder
1/2 cup grated skim-milk cheese,
  1% fat (maximum)

Place the vegetables, stock, and seasoning into a saucepan. Bring to the boil, and simmer for 20 minutes only.

Thicken with the cornflour. Add the skim-milk powder. Place mixture into an ovenproof casserole dish. Top with the grated cheese and bake in a moderate oven for 45 minutes.

Serves 4–6.

Variation

Add 1 tablespoon tomato paste (low salt), or 1 tomato.

Vegetable patties

3 cups cooked potato, dry-mashed
1 small onion, diced
2 cups dry mixed vegetables, cooked

Unprocessed bran for coating
Pinch each basil, oregano, sage
Pinch cayenne pepper

Combine the potato, onion and cooked mixed vegetables, make spoonfuls into patties, and flatten. Roll them in the unprocessed bran. Brown each on both sides in non-stick frying pan.

Serve hot with steamed vegetables or salad.

Serves 4.

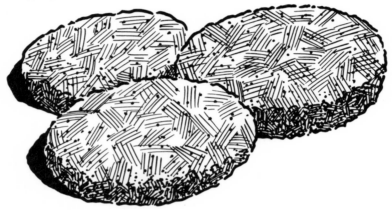

Vegetable pie

6 medium-sized potatoes, grated
6 medium-sized carrots, grated
1 large onion, finely chopped
1 clove garlic, crushed
2 egg whites (discard yolks)
¼ cup parsley, chopped (optional)
½ cup skim-milk powder

¼ cup breadcrumbs (approved bread)
½ cup grated cheese, 1% fat (maximum)
1 cup non-fat yoghurt, sugar free
4 shallots, chopped

Mix the potatoes, carrots, onion, and garlic. Lightly beat the egg white and pour it over the vegetables. Stir in the parsley, milk, and breadcrumbs. Pour into an ovenproof pie dish. Bake in a moderate oven for 4–5 minutes. Sprinkle with the grated cheese. Return to oven for 15 minutes more.

Serve hot, topped with the yoghurt mixed with the shallots. Serve with salad.

Serves 2–4.

Vegetable stew

1 medium-sized potato, cut into small cubes
1 carrot, cut into rings
1 small onion, sliced
½ cup fresh corn off the cob
2 medium-sized mushrooms sliced

½ cup fresh beans, chopped
Pinch each sage, garlic powder, basil and cayenne pepper
1 tablespoon tomato paste, low salt
½ cup stock, fat free (or water)
1 tablespoon cornflour

Place all the ingredients into a saucepan, except the cornflour, and simmer for 10 to 15 minutes only. Thicken with the cornflour mixed to a paste with water. Serve hot.

Serves 1.

This meal is tasty and filling. To serve more than one, increase the ingredients.

Variation

Use any of your favourite vegetables, but always include potato and carrot.

45

Welsh rarebit

4 slices approved bread
1/4 cup ricotta cheese, 1% fat
   (maximum) or non-fat

1 tomato, sliced
1/2 cup grated cheese, 1% fat
   (maximum)

Toast each of the slices of bread and spread lightly with the ricotta cheese.
Top with the slices of tomato and then the grated cheese. Place under the
griller and brown.
   Serve hot.
   Serves 4.

Zucchini pancakes

1/2 cup stoneground wholemeal
   flour
2 egg whites (discard yolks)

1/4 cup parsley, chopped
1/2 cup liquid skim milk
1/4 cup water

Filling

3 zucchini, sliced
1 medium-sized carrot, grated
1/2 cup grated cheese, 1% fat
   (maximum)

1/4 teaspoon nutmeg

Sauce

1 can tomatoes, drained and mashed
3 shallots

1/4 cup grated cheese, 1% fat
   (maximum)

Prepare the pancake ingredients and make eight pancakes. Leave in a
warm oven.
   Sauté all the filling ingredients in a non-stick frying pan, and divide into
eight portions.
   Place the portions on to the pancakes. Roll each pancake firmly. Place in
an ovenproof dish.
   Sauté the tomatoes and shallots for 15 minutes. Pour this over the
pancakes, and top with the grated cheese.
   Place the dish under the griller, and grill the cheese until it has melted.
   Serves 8.

Main dishes with meat, fish, or poultry

The tasty dishes in this section include main dishes similar to those you probably ate before you began to follow the Pritikin principles. Many favourite ingredients are used, such as soy sauce, curry powder, herbs and spices, mushrooms, onions, garlic, vegetables, and fruit.

You will find the meat, fish, or poultry are used as flavouring.

These points are essential:
* trim off all fat before cooking
* remove skin and bones before cooking
* flake salmon or tuna from cans, remove the skin and bones, and wash the fish under the tap to remove the brine
* grind your own hamburger mince from lean beef
* steam meat, fish, or poultry whenever possible before using it for a recipe
* use paper towelling to pat the meat, fish, or poultry after cooking and before serving
* use an electric knife to slice thinly
* never eat meat from a barbecue unless it is a lean piece with the fat trimmed off and then barbecued in foil.

RD   Use *only* the recipes in the previous section, Main Dishes with Vegetables or remember 100 gm or 3½ oz *per week* maximum.

MD   Allow 100 grams of lean meat, fish, or poultry a day. This may be a combination of all three.

Apricot chicken casserole

1 chicken, skinned and all fat
  removed, and cut into portions
1 large onion, sliced
2 carrots, sliced
2 large potatoes, sliced
3/4 cup corn, preferably fresh

3/4 cup peas, preferably fresh
1 clove garlic, crushed
1 large can apricots, unsweetened
1/2 cup apricot juice, unsweetened
2 tablespoons cornflour

Prepare the chicken pieces, onion, carrots and potatoes and place them in a casserole dish, the potatoes on the top. Blend the apricots, juice and cornflour (mixed with a little water) in a food processor. Pour this over the ingredients. Cover with the lid and bake in a moderate oven for about 2 hours or until the meat is tender.
  Serves 6–8.

Beef casserole

400 g lean round beef, fat removed
1 cup button mushrooms, sliced
1/2 green pepper (optional)
1 small diced onion
1 cup steamed carrot rings

3/4 cup cooked peas
1/2 cup skim-milk liquid
1/4 teaspoon nutmeg
1 tablespoon tomato paste
1 tablespoon cornflour

Cut the beef into four pieces and steam it for 5 minutes to remove any fat. Drain, and dry with paper towels. Brown in a non-stick pan. Arrange in a casserole dish. Add the mushroom, pepper, onion, carrot and peas. Mix the skim milk, nutmeg, tomato paste, and cornflour mixed with water, and pour over the meat and vegetables.
  Cover and gently simmer in a moderate oven for 30 minutes.
  Serve with wholemeal cooked noodles and green salad.
  Serves 4.

Cubed beef with prunes (MD) (page 51) served with Potatoes in yoghurt (RD) (page 34).

Beef fricassee

MD

400 g lean round beef, fat removed
2 medium-sized onions, cut into
  pieces
1½ cups chicken stock, fat free
2 tablespoons lemon juice

2 medium-sized carrots, cut in chunks
¼ cup skim-milk powder
1 tablespoon cornflour
Pinch nutmeg
Pinch garlic powder

Cut the beef into small pieces. Combine all the ingredients except the skim-milk powder and cornflour. Simmer gently until the meat is tender. Mix the skim-milk powder and cornflour in water, and thicken the mixture.
Serves 4.

Variation

Use 1 cup chicken pieces, fat and skin removed, instead of beef.

Chicken and grape casserole

MD

4 small chicken breasts, fat and
  skin removed
2 medium-sized onions, cut into
  rings
½ cup chicken stock, fat free

1 cup unsweetened apple juice
1 teaspoon soy sauce, low salt
18 large grapes, seeds removed
Pinch garlic powder
1 teaspoon cornflour

Brown the chicken breasts on both sides in a non-stick pan. Sauté the onions in a little chicken stock—do not burn. Add the chicken breasts, garlic, apple juice, and chicken stock. Mix the cornflour in water, add the soy sauce, and thicken the mixture. Pour gently into the casserole dish. Add the washed grapes. Cover with the lid and gently simmer in a moderate oven for about 30 minutes.
Serves 4.

From top left: Banana cream dessert (RD) (page 60), Cherry sago (RD) (page 69) topped with Exchange cream (RD) (page 84), California salad (RD) (page 61) topped with Exchange cream (RD) (page 84), and Pineapple boats (RD) (page 65).

MD ## Chicken and mushroom casserole

1½ cups diced chicken, fat free
1 cup mushrooms, sliced
1 small onion, chopped
½ cup chicken stock, fat free

½ cup liquid skim milk
1½ cups breadcrumbs (Pritikin or
approved bread)

Gently mix all the ingredients and place them in an ovenproof casserole dish. Bake for 1 hour in a moderate oven.
Serves 4.

MD ## Chicken with mango sauce

4 small chicken breasts, skin and
fat removed

1 medium-sized onion, sliced
1 stick celery, chopped

Sauce
1 mango, seeds and peel removed
½ teaspoon lemon rind, grated
1 tablespoon lemon juice
⅓ cup chicken stock, fat free

¼ cup liquid skim milk
Pinch garlic powder
1 tablespoon cornflour

Brown both sides of the chicken breasts in a non-stick pan. Sauté the onion and celery, but do not brown. Blend the prepared mango to pulp, add to the remaining ingredients and thicken with the cornflour mixed with water. Pour over the chicken breasts. Serve hot.
Serves 4.

Cubed beef with prunes

MD

400 g cubed non-fat beef, fat and
* skin removed*
10 prunes
1 cup unsweetened apple juice
1 tablespoon stoneground
* wholemeal flour*

1 large onion, chopped
2 tablespoons tomato paste, low salt
2 cups canned tomatoes, salt free
1 tablespoon cornflour
Pinch each basil and sage

Soak the prunes in the apple juice for 1 hour. Toss the meat in the flour
and brown with the onions in a non-stick frying pan. Add the prunes,
apple juice, and tomato paste.

Place into a casserole dish with the tomatoes. Thicken with the cornflour
mixed with a little water. Add the herbs. Add extra water if necessary.

Cover the casserole dish and gently simmer in a moderate oven until the
meat is tender.

Serves 4.

Curried chicken with apricots

MD

4 small chicken breasts, skin and
* fat removed*
¼ cup stoneground wholemeal flour
1 teaspoon curry powder
Pinch garlic powder
1 white onion, minced

1 cup button mushrooms, sliced
2 cups liquid skim milk
1 tablespoon cornflour
1 tablespoon Date Purée (page 83)
8 apricot halves, drained and
* unsweetened*

Coat the chicken breasts in the seasoned flour. Gently brown on both
sides in a non-stick frying pan. Add the onion and mushroom. Sauté for a
few minutes.

Transfer to an overproof dish. Pour over the skim milk mixed with the
cornflour and a little water, and Date Purée. Cover with the lid and gently
bake in a moderate oven for about 1 hour. Fifteen minutes before serving,
top with the apricot halves. Serve with brown rice.

Serves 4.

MD   # Curried salmon

220 g can pink or red salmon
1 medium-sized onion, chopped
1 medium-sized carrot, cut in discs
2 cups stock, fat free, (or water)
1 cup cooked peas
¼ cup skim-milk powder
¼–1 teaspoon curry powder

1 tablespoon cornflour
½ cup breadcrumbs (Pritikin or
 approved bread)
½ cup grated cheese, 1% fat
 (maximum)
2 cups cooked brown rice

Sauté the onion and carrot in a little of the stock for 10 minutes. Add the remaining stock and peas. Remove the skin and bones from the salmon. Gently wash the fish under water to remove the brine. Fold it into the mixture. Thicken with the skim milk, curry powder and cornflour mixed with water.

Pour on to a bed of brown rice in a casserole dish. Top with the breadcrumbs and grated cheese.

Bake in a moderate oven for 20 to 30 minutes until topping is lightly browned. Serve hot.

Serves 4.

MD   # Irish stew

Four 100 g pieces lean round beef,
 fat removed
4 medium-sized potatoes, peeled
 and quartered

2 medium-sized onions, sliced in
 rings
1 cup stock, fat free
1 bay leaf

Steam the meat to remove fat. Then place all the ingredients into a saucepan. Gently simmer them for 2 hours, until the stew is thick and the meat is tender.

Serves 4.

Salmon bake

Filling

2 cups cooked brown rice
1/4 cup parsley, chopped
2 egg whites (discard yolks)
2 x 220 g cans pink or red salmon

1 cup cooked silver beet, chopped
1/2 cup spring onions, chopped
1 red or green pepper, chopped

Topping

1 cup non-fat yoghurt, sugar free
1 egg white (discard yolk)
1 cup skim-milk liquid

1/2 cup grated cheese, 1% fat
  (maximum)

Mix the rice, parsley and beaten egg white, and press the mixture into an
ovenproof dish. Remove the skin and bones of the salmon. Flake, and
wash under water to remove the brine.

Arrange layers of the silver beet, salmon, onion and pepper on top of
the rice base.

Mix together the yoghurt, beaten egg white and skim milk. Gently pour
this over the salmon mixture. Sprinkle with the grated cheese. Bake in
moderate oven for about 40 minutes. Serve with garden salad, or vegetables
of your choice.

Serves 4–6.

Variation

Use one can of tuna instead of salmon. Prepare as above.

MD # Salmon patties

220 g can pink or red salmon
4 medium-sized potatoes, cooked
  and dry-mashed

1 small onion, diced (optional)
Unprocessed bran

Remove the skin and bones from the salmon. Wash the flesh under water to remove the brine. Mix the fish into the mashed potato and make spoonfuls into medium-sized patties. Roll each of the patties in the unprocessed bran, and flatten.

Brown each side of the patties in a non-stick frying pan. Serve with hot vegetables or salad.

Serves 4.

MD # Sweet and sour fish

2 cups whiting
1 medium-sized onion, diced
1 clove garlic, crushed
1 red pepper, chopped

1 green pepper, chopped
1 stick celery, chopped
450 g can pineapple pieces,
  unsweetened — save juice for sauce

Sauce

3/4 cup liquid from pineapple
  juice and water
1/2 cup white vinegar

1/2 cup pitted dates, chopped
1 tablespoon soy sauce, low salt
1 tablespoon cornflour

Remove the skin and bones from the fish and cut into small pieces. Sauté the onion and garlic in a little pineapple juice until tender. Add the peppers, celery, and pineapple pieces. Cook for about 1 minute. Add the fish.

Mix together all the sauce ingredients. Place this in a saucepan and bring to the boil. Gently simmer until the dates dissolve. Gently fold this into the fish and vegetables. Serve hot on a bed of cooked brown rice.

Serves 4.

Sweet and sour meatballs

MD

220 g home-minced, low-fat beef
¼ cup carrot, grated
1 small onion, finely diced

½ cup cooked brown rice
1 egg white (discard yolk)
Unprocessed bran

Sauce

½ cup vinegar
1 tablespoon soy sauce, low salt
½ cup Date Purée (page 83)
⅓ cup pineapple juice, unsweetened

1 tablespoon cornflour
1 cup unsweetened pineapple pieces
1 small green pepper, chopped

Mix the beef, vegetables, rice, and egg white. Form into tiny meatballs.
Coat these with the unprocessed bran. Gently brown all over in a non-stick frying pan.

To make the sauce, mix the vinegar, soy sauce, purée and ⅓ cup pineapple juice in a saucepan and bring to the boil. Thicken with the cornflour and juice. Add the pineapple pieces and chopped pepper. Pour the sauce over the meatballs.

Serve hot on a bed of cooked brown rice.

Serves 4.

Virginia roast (1)

Virginia roast is the piece of beef taken from the hind leg of the beast. It should not be confused either with Virginia ham or pork, neither of which is acceptable due to their high cholesterol and fat content.

400 g Virginia roast, fat and skin   *1 clove garlic, crushed*
removed   *Small quantity water*

Place the meat in a saucepan with the water and the crushed garlic. Gently simmer it until the meat is tender. Slice the 'roast' very thinly.

Gently pat the slices with paper towels. Serve with roast potatoes (page 32), steamed vegetables, and one of my gravies (pages 82–92).
Serves 4.

Virginia roast (2)

This baked dinner is permitted occasionally. But the guidelines regarding the eating of meat must be observed. Serve fat free and skinned meat, making sure that no more than the allowance is served on to your plate.

400 g Virginia roast, fat and
skin removed
1 roasting bag (or aluminium foil)

Preheat oven to 200°C.

Place the meat in a bag or wrap it in foil. Place it on a wire rack in the roasting dish. Bake in a pre-heated oven until the meat is tender and cooked.

Fruit desserts

Fruit, rich in vitamins and minerals, is the better for you if it is organically grown, eaten fresh, and in season.

Try to buy apples and other fruit that have unwaxed skins, and eat strawberries sparingly because they contribute to raised uric acid levels.

If you follow the Regression Diet, remember that you must adhere strictly to three pieces of fruit daily. No dried fruit is allowed. But, with a little flair and imagination, you can eat a variety of fruit.

The Maintenance Diet allows five pieces of fruit daily—as well as dried fruit, naturally dried if possible (the colour is darker). The types of fruit eaten daily may be varied, providing that your triglyceride reading remains within the Pritikin recommended range.

RD

Apricot dessert

1 cup apricots (in natural juice),
  chopped
2 teaspoons apricot juice
2 tablespoons unsweetened apple
  juice

1¼ cups ricotta cheese, 1% fat
  (maximum) or non-fat
4 drained apricot halves as garnish

Gently mix the apricots and juices. Whip the cheese and very gently fold
it into the chopped apricots and juice. Garnish with the apricots. Serve
chilled.
  Serves 4.

Variation

RD

Pineapple may be substituted for apricots. Garnish with strawberries.

MD

Baked apples

4 medium-sized cooking apples,
  cored
4 dates, pitted and chopped

½ cup Date Purée (page 83)
½ cup water
Grated orange peel

Wash and core the apples (leave the skin on). Fill the apples with the
chopped dates. Pour over the combined liquids and peel. Bake in a
moderate oven for about 1 hour. Serve hot.
  Serves 4.

Variations

1. Use ¼ cup natural sultanas instead of dates.
2. Use natural unsweetened grape juice instead of Date Purée and water.

Baked apples with apricots

4 medium-sized cooking apples,
  cored and peeled
1 cup apricots in natural juice,
  chopped

Lemon juice and a little water
1 cup apricot juice, unsweetened
1 tablespoon fresh orange juice
1 teaspoon orange rind

Stand the apples upright in a little water and simmer them with the lemon juice for 15 minutes only. Drain and remove the apples. Fill the centres with the chopped apricots, and pour the combined remaining liquids and the orange rind over the apples.

Bake in a moderate oven, and baste frequently with the liquid for about 15 minutes. Remove the apples from the oven, and continue to baste as they cool. Serve warm.

Serves 4.

Baked bananas

4 whole bananas, peeled
8 tablespoons fresh orange juice
4 teaspoons fresh lemon juice

Place the bananas in a baking dish and pour the juice over them. Bake in a hot oven for 10 to 15 minutes.

Serves 4

Baked ginger pears

6 ripe whole pears (firm to touch),
  with stem on
3/4 cup unsweetened apple juice
1 teaspoon ground ginger
2 teaspoons lemon juice

1 tablespoon lemon peel, cut into
  thin strips
3 teaspoons sago
6 mint leaves, to decorate

Gently simmer all the ingredients, except the pears and mint leaves, for
5 minutes only. Arrange the pears upright in a baking dish. Pour the
liquid over the pears, cover, and bake for about 40 minutes in a moderate
oven. Baste during cooking. Garnish with the mint leaves. Serve at once.
  Serves 4–6.

Banana cream dessert

3 ripe bananas
2 teaspoons lemon juice
2 tablespoons unsweetened apple
  juice

1 1/4 cups ricotta cheese, 1% fat
  (maximum) or non-fat

Mash the bananas with the lemon and apple juice. Whip the cheese and
fold it into the banana mixture. Spoon into glass dishes. Serve chilled.
  Serves 4.

Bananas with crepes

MD

Crepes

¾ cup stoneground wholemeal flour
½ cup liquid skim milk

½ cup water
2 egg whites (discard yolks)

Topping

3 bananas, sliced
½ cup dates, pitted and chopped
1 cup unsweetened orange juice

2 tablespoons lemon juice
1 teaspoon lemon rind, grated

Simmer the dates, juices and rind until the mixture is thick and the dates are soft and smooth. Add the sliced bananas. Heat through and serve over the warm crepes. Serve with Exchange Cream (1), page 84.

Serves 4–6.

California salad

RD

2 cups sultana grapes, or large
  grapes, seeds removed
2 cups fresh or unsweetened
  pineapple, chopped

½ cup pineapple juice, sugar free
¼ teaspoon ground ginger

Wash and drain the grapes, cut and prepare the pineapple. Mix them together with the ginger. Leave for several hours. Serve chilled.

Top with Exchange Cream (1) on page 84.

Serves 4.

61

Carob mousse

2 tablespoons carob powder
2 tablespoons water to mix carob
½ 440 g can chestnut purée
1 egg white (discard yolk)
½ cup skim-milk powder

1 cup water
2 teaspoons gelatine
2 tablespoons warm water to mix
  gelatine

Mix the carob powder in the 2 tablespoons of water until smooth. Place the carob paste, chestnut purée, egg white, skim-milk powder and cup of water into a blender. Blend until smooth.

Mix the gelatine with the water until dissolved. Add to the blender and mix with the other ingredients.

Pour into long glasses. Chill in the fridge until set. Garnish with Exchange Cream (page 84) and strawberry halves.
Serves 2–3.

MD

Cheese cake

Crumb crust
(line base with tin foil)
¾ cup crumbed muesli (or
  crumbed oatmeal)
2 teaspoons grated orange peel

1 teaspoon cinnamon
Small amount of natural
  unsweetened grape juice

Filling
500 g low-fat cottage cheese
2 egg whites (discard yolks)
3 teaspoons lemon peel
¼ cup evaporated skim milk
3 teaspoons gelatine

3 tablespoons hot water to mix
  gelatine
1 tablespoon Date Purée (page 83)
3 tablespoons natural apple juice,
  sugar free

Topping
1½ cups berry fruit of your choice,
  mashed

To make the crumb crust, combine the muesli, peel and cinnamon. With the grape juice, make the crust moist enough to press on to a spring-form base lined with foil. Bake in a moderate oven for 10 minutes only. Cool.

To make the filling, dissolve the gelatine in the hot water. Cool. Mix with all the other ingredients in a blender until smooth. Pour this on to the biscuit base and chill. When set, decorate with the washed berries.

Variation

RD   Omit Date Purée.

Cooked prunes

MD

1 cup prunes
½ cup natural grape juice,
  unsweetened
Lemon peel

Bring all the ingredients to the boil and gently simmer them until the prunes are soft. Chill and serve.
  Serves 2.

Fresh fruit kebabs

12 pieces fresh pineapple
12 fresh strawberries, hulled
2 medium-sized bananas, in small

slices (about 4 cm)
2 kiwi fruit, peeled and quartered

Marinade

1 cup unsweetened apple juice
Juice 1 orange

Pinch cinnamon
1 tablespoon brandy (optional)

You will also need 4 metal skewers.

Prepare the fruit and soak in the marinade for several hours. Drain the fruit just before serving. Place it decoratively on to each of the four skewers. Wrap in foil and place over a barbecue flame for several seconds, turning them all the time. Serve hot with one of the fruit exchange creams (page 86).
   Serves 4.

Variation

RD

Follow the above method, but omit one of the fruits and brandy. Serve with Exchange Cream (1) or Exchange Cream (2) (page 84).

RD

Fresh fruit salad

1 cup fresh pineapple pieces
2 oranges, peeled and diced
1 red apple, diced, skin left on
1 green apple, diced, skin left on
2 bananas, sliced
1 peach, diced (fresh or natural
  juice, sugar free)

1 pear, diced, skin left on
2 passionfruit
1 kiwi fruit, sliced
Juice of 3 oranges

Combine all the ingredients, except the kiwi fruit, in a glass bowl. Decorate with the kiwi fruit.
   If you are keeping fruit salad for any length of time, add banana just prior to serving so that it won't go soggy and discolour.
   Serves 2–3.

Variations

Use combinations of your favourite fruits, but limit the use of strawberries.

Festive Christmas cake (MD) (page 72) and Grape juice punch (page 104).

64

Oranges in date sauce

4 medium-sized sweet oranges,
  whole
1¼ cups unsweetened apple juice or
  orange juice

½ cup Date Purée (page 83)
½ cup orange peel strips, long and
  fine

Peel the oranges, cut away the pith, and leave them whole. Soak the orange peel in the apple juice for 1 hour. Then add the date purée and gently simmer for about ½ hour.

Place the oranges in a deep small dish and gently pour the sauce over the oranges. At least 2 hours before serving, baste with the syrup. Top with the peel.

Serves 4.

Variation

As above, but slice the oranges instead of using them whole.

Pineapple boats

1 pineapple, cut into 4 lengthwise
1 cup strawberries, hulled and
  halved (leave 4 for garnish)
1 cup cantelope balls
1 cup watermelon balls

¼ teaspoon ground ginger
2 tablespoons orange juice, fresh
2 cartons chunky fruit yoghurt,
  1% fat (maximum)

Scoop out the pineapple and cut into chunks. Combine the fruit, ginger, and orange juice. Spoon into the pineapple boats. Pour the yoghurt over, and garnish each with strawberries.

Serves 4.

From left: Sultana ginger loaf (MD) (page 75), Sweet potato scones (RD) (page 80) with Raspberry spread (RD) (page 90) and Exchange cream (1) (RD) (page 84), Helene's date balls (MD) (page 72) and Approved herb tea (RD).

MD # Stewed rhubarb

2 cups rhubarb, cut up
½ cup dates, pitted and chopped
1 cup natural grape juice, sugar free

Place all the ingredients in a saucepan and gently simmer until cooked.
Serve chilled, or use in a fruit pie, or combine with stewed apples.
   Serves 2–3.

MD # Yoghurt prunes

1 cup prunes (no juice), cooked   *1 cup non-fat yoghurt, sugar free*
and pitted   *1 tablespoon Date Purée (page 83)*

Chop the prunes. Mix the prunes, yoghurt and purée gently together and
serve in individual glasses.
   Serves 2.

Cakes and puddings

These recipes are very easy to prepare if you carefully follow the instructions. The results will be delicious.

Your cakes may be decorated with cracked wheat, if you wish, or, very sparingly, with poppy or sesame seeds.

If you buy fruit juice, make sure that it does not contain preservatives, sweetening, colouring or other artificial flavouring, or other additives.

RD ## Apple pie

4 cooking apples, peeled and sliced
2 cloves
1/3 cup unsweetened apple juice
Quantity of Sweet Wholemeal
  Pastry (page 110)

Small quantity of non-fat yoghurt,
  sugar free

Preheat the oven to moderate.

Prepare and place the apples, cloves and liquid into a non-stick pan with a lid. Constantly turn and simmer them for about 10 minutes. *Do not brown.* Cool.

Prepare the pastry and line the bottom of a pie dish. Pour in the apple mixture. Top with the remaining pastry. Brush the top with the yoghurt and put little slits in the top of the pastry. Cook in the oven for about 30 minutes.

Serve warm with Exchange Cream (page 84) or White Sauce (page 92).

Variation

MD As above, but add 1/2 cup natural sultanas, or 1/2 cup chopped dates.

RD ## Apple rice pudding

1 apple, peeled and sliced thinly
1 cup cooked creamed brown rice
1 egg white, beaten (discard yolk)

1/4 teaspoon cinnamon
1 large can apricots in natural juice

Preheat the oven to 140°C.

Mix the rice and egg white and put into a shallow ovenproof dish. Arrange the thinly sliced apple on top of the rice. Sprinkle the top of the apple with the cinnamon. Bake uncovered for 30 minutes. Serve with canned apricots.

Serves 4.

68

Bran muffins

1½ cups stoneground wholemeal SR
  flour
½ cup non-fat yoghurt, sugar free
¼ cup unprocessed bran
1 cup natural sultanas

¼ cup skim-milk powder
1 egg white (discard yolk)
½ cup unsweetened apple or
  grape juice

Preheat the oven to moderate.
    Combine all the ingredients until the mixture resembles cake consistency.
Place spoonfuls into non-stick muffin tins. Bake in the oven for 15 to 20
minutes until brown.
    Makes about 9.

Cherry sago

5 cups fresh cherries
¾ cup sago

1½ cups water
3½ cups water

Soak the sago in the 1½ cups water for 2 to 3 hours and drain. Place the
cherries into a saucepan with the 3½ cups of water and bring to the boil.
Add the drained sago and gently simmer until the cherries are tender and
the sago is clear.
    Serves 4–6.

Christmas pudding

½ cup natural sultanas
½ cup natural raisins, chopped
½ cup dates, pitted and chopped
¼ cup currants, undipped * in
  sulphur
¼ cup brandy
½ cup stoneground wholemeal SR
  flour

1 teaspoon mixed spice
½ teaspoon nutmeg
2 egg whites (discard yolks)
¾ cup skim-milk liquid
Rind 1 orange, grated
Rind 1 lemon, grated

Soak the fruit in the brandy overnight. Next day, mix the dry ingredients
and egg whites with a little of the skim milk. Then alternately add the fruit
and milk to make a moist cake consistency. Add the grated rind.
    Place into a foil lined steamer and gently steam for 3 hours.
    Serve hot with Brandy Sauce (page 83).

---

* These are obtainable from Health Food Stores.

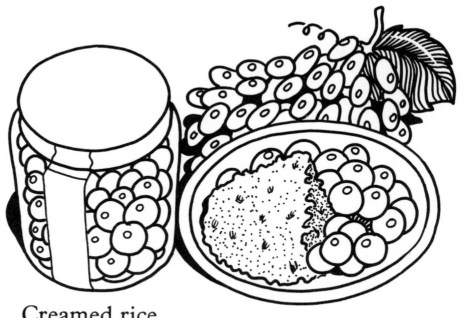

RD   Creamed rice

1 cup brown rice – biodynamic if   3 cups cold water
*   possible   ¼ cup skim-milk powder*

Place the rice and water in a saucepan. Bring to the boil and gently simmer until the rice is thick and swollen. Add more water if necessary. When the rice is cooked, add the skim-milk powder (mixed with some water) and stir into rice. Serve hot or cold.
   Serves 3–4.

Variation

Place the rice and water into the top of a double saucepan and slowly cook it until the rice is fluffy. Add the skim-milk powder (mixed with water). Serve hot or cold.

MD   Creamed rice, sweet

Add ½ cup natural sultanas to the
*   ingredients for Creamed Rice.*

Follow the same method. If you like, serve the rice with your favourite stewed fruit, unsweetened.

70

Date cake

1 cup dates, pitted and chopped
1/2 cup yoghurt, non-fat and sugar
 free
2 cups stoneground wholemeal SR
 flour

1/2 cup grape juice, unsweetened
1 egg white (discard yolk)
Some liquid skim milk

Preheat the oven to very hot.

Place the dates and grape juice in saucepan and boil. Cool. Blend together the yoghurt and egg white. Add this to the flour and fold the mixture into the date mixture.

Mix to a cake consistency. Use some of the skim milk if the mixture is dry. Pour the mixture into a foil-lined log tin.

Place the cake in the oven, reduce the temperature to 180°C, and cook for 30 to 45 minutes.

Cool in an airtight tin.

Variations

1. Pumpkin cake: Add 1/2 cup cold cooked pumpkin.
2. Sultana cake: Substitute 3/4 cup natural sultanas for the dates.
3. Mixed fruit: Substitute 1 cup mixed fruit for the dates — e.g. natural sultanas, raisins, dates and currants. Add 1/2 teaspoon mixed spice, 1/4 teaspoon powdered ginger, and 1/4 teaspoon nutmeg.

Easy moist fruit cake

1 1/2 cups dates, soft and pitted
1 cup natural sultanas
1/2 cup water
2 cups stoneground wholemeal SR
 flour

1/2 cup unprocessed bran
1 egg white (discard yolk)
Some liquid skim milk

Preheat the oven to moderate.

Cook the dates and sultanas in the water, and cool. Add the remaining ingredients and mix to a cake consistency, using some skim milk.

Pour into a foil-lined log tin and bake in the oven for 45 to 60 minutes.

Festive Christmas cake

1 cup natural raisins, chopped
1½ cups natural sultanas
1½ cups undipped currants
⅓ cup mixed peel, soaked 1 hour in
 boiling water to remove sugar
8 chopped glacé cherries, soaked
 1 hour in boiling water to remove
 sugar
1 cup dates, pitted and chopped
1 tablespoon whisky (optional)
1 cup dark unsweetened grape juice

1½ cups stoneground wholemeal SR
 flour
⅓ cup unprocessed bran
2 tablespoons Pineapple Ginger
 Spread (page 88)
3 egg whites (discard yolks)
A little egg white to brush top of cake
1 teaspoon nutmeg
1 teaspoon cinnamon
½ cup liquid skim milk

Preheat the oven to moderate.

Prepare all the fruit and soak it overnight, covered, in the whisky and grape juice. Next day, mix together all the other ingredients, and slowly add the skim-milk liquid. Fold in prepared fruit and place in a non-stick cake tin, 20 cm in diameter, which has the bottom lined with two thicknesses of greaseproof paper.

Bake the cake for 1 hour, then reduce the temperature to slow for a further 30 to 45 minutes. Place the cooked cake in an airtight tin for 15 minutes for easy removal. Decorate with holly.

Helene's date balls

2 cups soft pitted dates
2 cups rolled oats, sugar free (not
 instant)

2 tablespoons lemon juice

Place ½ cup of the oats in a food processor and grind them until they resemble fine crumbs. Put aside. Add the remaining ingredients to the processor and blend (but not too finely).

Work spoonfulls of the mixture into small balls with your hands. Coat with the crumbed rolled oats. Store in refrigerator in container.
Makes about 24.

Old-fashioned date loaf

MD

⅓ cup dates, pitted and chopped
1 cup Date Purée made with water
  (page 83)
⅓ cup unprocessed bran
1½ cups stoneground wholemeal SR
  flour

½ cup water
1 egg white (discard yolk)
¼ teaspoon cinnamon
¼ teaspoon nutmeg

Preheat the oven to 250°C.

Mix all the ingredients thoroughly. Spoon the mixture into a non-stick upright nutloaf tin. Cover with the lid. Stand the tin in the oven.

Reduce the temperature to 200°C and bake for 45 minutes.

Remove the tin from the oven and place it in an airtight tin for easy removal after 15 to 20 minutes.

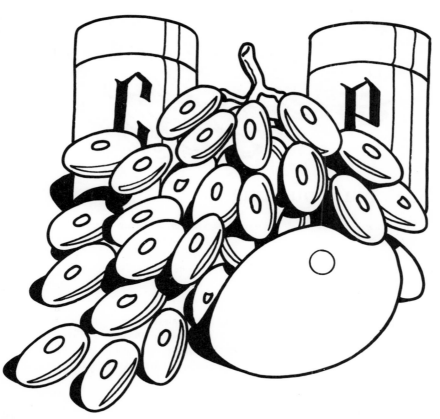

Quick fruit pudding

*1 cup stoneground wholemeal SR
flour*
*1½ cups mixed fruit — natural
sultanas, dates, raisins, and
currants*

1 tablespoon unprocessed bran
½ cup unsweetened grape juice
1 cup skim-milk liquid
1 teaspoon mixed spice
1 teaspoon nutmeg

Combine all the ingredients in a saucepan, except the flour. Bring to the
boil for 10 minutes, then cool. When cool, add the flour. Pour the mixture
into a steamer and gently simmer for 1½ hours. Serve hot.
  Serves 3–4.

Sago plum pudding

1 cup natural sultanas
½ cup sago
*½ cup natural grape juice,
  unsweetened*
1 cup stoneground wholemeal flour
¼ cup unprocessed bran

*¼ cup soft breadcrumbs (Pritikin
  or approved bread)*
1 egg white (discard yolk)
½ cup liquid skim milk
Extra skim milk

Soak the sago in the skim milk overnight. Mix all the ingredients together
to make a cake consistency. Use the extra milk if necessary. Place the
mixture into a steamer and steam for 1½ hours. Serve hot with White
Sauce (made with water) (page 92) or Exchange Cream (page 84).
  Serves 3–4.

Scotch pancakes

1 cup stoneground wholemeal SR
flour

1 egg white (discard yolk)
3/4 cup liquid skim milk

Mix all the ingredients until smooth. Drop spoonfulls in to a non-stick frying pan. Brown both sides. Top with one of my spreads, or mashed banana.

Variation

Ingredients and method as above. Add 1/4 cup natural sultanas to mixture.

Sultana ginger loaf

1/2 cup natural sultanas
1 1/2 cups stoneground wholemeal SR
flour
3 pieces chopped ginger, soaked in
boiling water for 1/2 hour and
washed to remove sugar

1 egg white (discard yolk)
3/4 cup unsweetened apple juice
1/2 cup skim-milk liquid
Pinch nutmeg
Pinch cinnamon

Preheat the oven to 250°C.

Place all the ingredients into a bowl and thoroughly mix them. Spoon the mixture into an upright non-stick nutloaf tin. Place the lid on top. Stand it upright in the oven.

Reduce the temperature to 200°C. Bake for 45 minutes.

Remove the tin from the oven and place it into an airtight tin for easy removal after 15 to 20 minutes.

Variations

1. Omit chopped ginger.
2. Substitute grape juice or fresh orange juice for unsweetened apple juice.
3. Add 3/4 cup of mixed natural sultanas, natural raisins and undipped currants. Omit the ginger.

Very moist pumpkin-prune cake

½ cup cooked cold pumpkin
1 cup cooked prunes, pitted and
chopped
1 egg white (discard yolk)
2½ cups stoneground wholemeal SR
flour

½ teaspoon each cloves, cinnamon
and ground ginger
1⅓ cups liquid skim milk

Preheat the oven to 250°C.

Blend the pumpkin, prunes and egg white in a blender (use the mixing blade). Pour over the flour and spices. Add the skim milk and mix. Pour into a foil-lined log tin and place in the oven.

Reduce the heat to 200°C and bake the cake for 45 minutes.

Yoghurt slice

1 cup yoghurt, non-fat and sugar
free
1 cup ricotta cheese, non-fat or
1% fat (maximum)
¼ cup uncreamed cottage cheese,
non-fat
Rind 1 lemon, grated
Lemon juice

2 egg whites (discard yolks)
2 tablespoons apple juice
2 cups Helene's Muesli (page 108) or
2 cups Oatmeal 'Crumb' Pastry
(page 109)
Small quantity unsweetened grape
juice to make a spreadable
biscuit mixture

Preheat the oven to moderate.

Make up the muesli, grind it, and press it into a foil-lined, 18 cm, non-stick cake tray or lamington tin. Blend all the other ingredients until soft and mixed. Pour the mixture on to the base and bake until firm. Cool and cut into slices.

Variation

MD Add ½ cup natural sultanas.
RD You may add ½ cup unsweetened fruit for added flavour.

Breads and scones

Breads and grains are an acceptable part of your diet and may be used liberally if you are not allergic to them. Many bakers make a variety of breads to the Pritikin principles. Your local baker may be prepared to bake bread using your own recipe.

Wholemeal pita bread and Lebanese bread are useful and may be used as a substitute for Pritikin bread. They may be:
- eaten with mashed bananas as a spread
- a base for home-made pizzas
- a substitute for lasagna pasta
- toasted and served in pieces as a substitute for savoury biscuits
- with soups or dips
- rolled up with salad inside
- topped with a favourite spread
- eaten plain if you are weight watching.

RD

Corn bread

¾ cup cornmeal – polenta
¼ cup stoneground wholemeal SR
 flour

1 teaspoon Date Purée (page 83)
¾ cup skim milk
1 egg white (discard yolk)

Preheat the oven to 200°C.

Vigorously mix all the ingredients, and fold into non-stick log tin. Bake 25 to 30 minutes until golden brown.

Serves 6.

RD

Scones

3 cups stoneground wholemeal SR
 flour
Skim-milk liquid

Extra stoneground wholemeal SR
 flour
A little non-fat yoghurt

Preheat the oven to 230°C.

Place the flour in a bowl. Gradually add the skim milk, stirring to make a scone dough. Gently knead on a floured board and press down to about 1 cm thick. With a scone cutter, cut into rounds. Brush the tops with some non-fat yoghurt. Place on a floured tray.

Reduce the temperature to 210°C. Bake for 10 to 15 minutes.

Remove from the oven and place in airtight tin or wrap in foil to keep them soft.

Serve with favourite toppings, or mashed banana, or eat whole with meals.

Variation

Pumpkin scones: Add ½ cup cold cooked pumpkin.

MD

Sweet scones: As above, add ¾ cup of natural sultanas, pitted chopped dates or mixture of dates, natural sultanas and chopped natural raisins.

78

Sue's cake bread

RD

1 cup stoneground wholemeal SR
 flour
¼ cup stoneground wholemeal flour
¼ cup uncooked brown rice
¼ cup rye flour

½ cup unprocessed bran
1 tablespoon millet
1 cup skim-milk liquid
or combinations of your own grains

Preheat the oven to moderate.

Place all the ingredients in a bowl and mix to a cake consistency. Pour into a foil lined log tin and bake for 1 hour. When cooked, place the cake bread in an airtight tin for about 30 to 60 minutes for easy removal of the foil.

Serve with favourite meals, or slice and spread with mashed banana or approved jams and spreads.

Variations

1. Substitute skim milk for unsweetened orange or pineapple juice.   RD
2. Carrot bread: Add ½ cup grated carrot.
3. Apple bread: Add ½ cup grated apple.

Fruit bread: Add ½ cup natural sultanas or currants, or dates, or a   MD
mixture of these fruits to ½ cup.

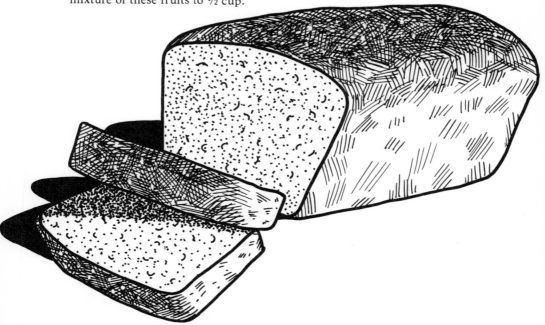

MD

Sweet potato scones

2 cups stoneground wholemeal SR
  flour
½ cup dry mashed potatoes
½ cup natural sultanas

½ cup skim-milk liquid
½ cup unsweetened apple juice
A little non-fat sugar free yoghurt

Preheat the oven to 230°C.

Mix all the ingredients together to form a dough. Gently knead it on a well floured board. Cut it into scone-sized rounds. Brush the tops with yoghurt.

Reduce the temperature to 220°C. Bake for 10 to 15 minutes.

These scones are very moist. Serve them with your favourite spread, or Exchange Cream (page 84) or eat plain.

Variation

RD   Omit the sultanas.

RD

Wally's bread

4 cups stoneground wholemeal SR
  flour

2 cups warm water
2 teaspoons yeast, dry

Preheat the oven to 200°C.

Place the 2 cups of warm water in a large bowl with the yeast. Add 2 cups of the flour and stir well, then add the remaining 2 cups of flour. It should be soft cake-type batter. If not, add a little more warm water to make the right consistency.

Place the mixture into a foil-lined bread tin and place in a warm position for 30 minutes. Then cook for 1 hour.

From top left: Raspberry spread (RD), Blackberry spread (RD), Apricot and pineapple spread (RD), Pineapple and ginger spread (RD), Tomato corn relish (MD) (pages 82–91), Wally's bread; rolls and loaves (RD) (page 80), Date scones (MD) (page 78), 1% fat ricotta cheese (RD).

Blackberry spread

Apricot and pineapple spread

Raspberry spread

Corn relish

Sauces, gravies, toppings, and spreads

There is no need to forego tasty sauces and gravies, salad dressings, sweet spreads and toppings, and so on, when you are following the diets. Use these to add interest to other dishes.

Bran muffins (MD) (page 69), Yoghurt slice with passionfruit (RD) (page 76), and Hot cappuccino exchange (RD) (page 105).

RD

Apricot and pineapple spread

1 cup unsweetened pineapple,
  chopped
1 cup unsweetened apricots,
  chopped

½ cup unsweetened apple juice

Place all the ingredients in a saucepan and gently simmer them for 20 minutes. Cook, and blend in a blender. Place in a sterilized glass jar and refrigerate.
  Makes 1 cup.

RD

Apricot ginger sauce

1 piece green ginger (size 50¢
  piece)
1 cup unsweetened apricot purée

3 teaspoons soy sauce, low salt
2 teaspoons cornflour
1 shallot, sliced

Finely chop the ginger, combine with the apricot purée and soy sauce. Bring to the boil and slowly add the cornflour mixed with water. Stir well until it thickens, with no lumps.
  Add the sliced shallot just before serving.
  Makes 1 cup.

RD

Apricot gravy

1 tablespoon cornflour
½ cup stock, non-fat
½ cup apricot purée

Mix the cornflour with a little water. Add it to the remaining ingredients in a saucepan and heat, stirring constantly, until thick.
  Makes 1 cup.

Variation

Tomato gravy: Omit the apricot purée. Add 1 tomato and 1 chopped onion. Prepare as above.

82

Blackberry spread

2 cups fresh blackberries
1 cup unsweetened dark grape juice

Place the ingredients in a saucepan. Gently simmer for 30 to 60 minutes. When the mixture is thick, cool it and store in sterilized jars in the refrigerator.
   Makes 1 cup.

Variation

Add ½ cup pitted, chopped dates.

MD

Brandy sauce

RD

1 tablespoon cornflour
1 cup water
2 tablespoons skim-milk powder

1 tablespoon brandy
1 tablespoon Date Purée (page 83)

Mix the cornflour with a little water. Add it to the remaining ingredients in a saucepan. Stir constantly until the mixture thickens. Add more cornflour for a thicker consistency.
   Makes 1 cup.

Date purée

MD

1 cup pitted dates
1¼ cups water (or grape juice)

Place the ingredients in a saucepan and simmer them until thick and the liquid absorbed. Blend in a blender. Use as a sweetener.
   Makes 1¾ cups.

Easy fruit jam

½ cup natural sultanas
½ cup pitted dates, chopped
¼ cup currants, undipped
¼ cup natural raisins, chopped

Pinch powdered ginger (optional)
½–1 cup natural unsweetened grape
   juice

Place all the ingredients in a saucepan and gently simmer them until they are soft. Place in a blender and blend. Put into a sterilized jar and store in the refrigerator. Use sparingly.
   Makes 1 cup.

Exchange cream (1)

½ cup ricotta cheese, non-fat or
   1% fat (maximum)
⅓ cup skim-milk powder

½ cup cold water
Drop of vanilla (optional)

Place all the ingredients in a blender and mix. Serve cold as a topping on desserts and puddings.
   Makes 2 cups.

Exchange cream (2)

½ cup skim-milk powder
¼ cup cold water
Drop of vanilla (optional)

Beat all the ingredients with an electric beater and place the bowl in the freezer for 10 minutes. Remove from the freezer and beat again. Repeat this procedure until the mixture is thick and frothy—about 30–45 minutes. Serve immediately on desserts and puddings.
   Makes 1½ cups.

French dressing

1/4 *cup vinegar – ordinary or cider*
1/4 *cup lemon juice*
1/4 *teaspoon dry mustard*

1/4 *teaspoon paprika*
Pinch garlic powder (optional)
2 *tablespoons wine vinegar*

Blend all the ingredients, and use over a salad.
Makes 1/2 cup.

Variation

Sweet French dressing: Add 1 teaspoon Date Purée (page 83).

Leek sauce

2 *leeks, thinly sliced*
1 *clove garlic, crushed*
1 1/2 *cups chicken stock, fat free*
1 *teaspoon French mustard*
2 *teaspoons chopped parsley*

1 *teaspoons lemon juice*
1 *tablespoon skim-milk powder*
2 *teaspoons grated cheese, 1% fat*
   (maximum)

Sauté the leeks and crushed garlic in a little of the stock until tender. Add the remaining stock, mustard and parsley and cook for 20 minutes. Blend in a blender. Add the remaining ingredients and simmer for 1 minute.
Makes 2 cups.

Lemon sauce for fish

1 *tablespoon lemon juice*
1 *cup chicken stock, fat free*

1 *tablespoon skim-milk powder*
2 *teaspoons cornflour*

Place all the ingredients in a saucepan, except the cornflour. Bring to the boil. Thicken with cornflour mixed with a little water. Gently simmer.
Makes 1 1/2 cups.

Loganberry spread

2 cups fresh loganberries
1 cup unsweetened dark grape juice

Place the ingredients in a saucepan. Gently simmer for 30 to 60 minutes. When the mixture is thick, cool it, and store in sterilized jars in the refrigerator.
   Makes 1 cup.

Variation

MD   Add ½ cup pitted, chopped dates.

RD

Mango cream exchange

1 cup ricotta cheese, non-fat or
 1% fat (maximum)
½ cup liquid skim milk

Pulp of 1 mango, seeds and skin
 removed

Place all the ingredients into a blender and blend them. Serve with fresh fruit combinations or over hot puddings.
   Makes 1 cup.

Variation

1. Apricot cream exchange: Substitute ½ cup chopped unsweetened apricots for the mango.
2. Passionfruit cream exchange: Omit the mango. Blend the ricotta cheese and skim milk, and *fold* in the pulp of 2 passionfruit.

Mayonnaise

½ cup yoghurt, non-fat
¼ cup ricotta cheese, non-fat or
  1% fat (maximum)
¼ cup non-fat uncreamed cottage
  cheese
3 tablespoons vinegar

Juice of 1 lemon
Pinch each garlic powder and
  onion powder
¼ teaspoon mustard powder
1 tablespoon Date Purée (page 83)
Some liquid skim milk

Put all the ingredients in a blender, add skim milk liquid to blend.
  Makes 1½ cups.

Variation

Thousand island dressing: Substitute 1 tablespoon tomato sauce for the
mustard powder. Blend in a blender.

Mushroom gravy

1 cup stock, non-fat
3 fresh mushrooms, chopped
1 tablespoon cornflour

1 teaspoon low-salt soy sauce
Pinch garlic powder (optional)

Mix the cornflour with a little water. Add to the remaining ingredients in
a saucepan and stir until thickened. Serve over the Virginia Roast
(page 56).
  Makes 1 cup.

Mushroom sauce

½ cup spring onions, chopped
1 cup button mushrooms, sliced
1 cup stock, fat free

1 tablespoon skim-milk powder
Pinch garlic powder
1 tablespoon cornflour

Toss the onions and mushrooms in a non-stick frying pan, and gently
brown. Add the stock, skim-milk powder, and garlic powder. Thicken
with the cornflour, mixed with a little water.
  Makes 1½ cups.

Non-fat Ricotta Cheese

RD

½ cup skim milk powder
2 cups cold water
1 tablespoon fresh lemon juice

You will also need muslin to
strain through.

Mix water and skim milk powder in saucepan and bring to boil—add lemon juice and stand aside for half an hour until cool. Strain through muslin to remove liquid.
  Makes about ½ cup of Ricotta Cheese.

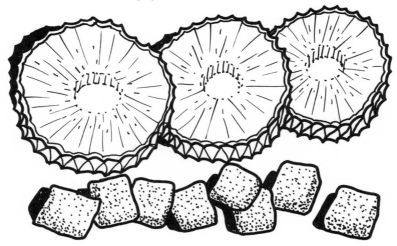

Pineapple and ginger spread

RD

1 cup unsweetened pineapple,
* chopped*
8 medium-sized pieces of
* crystallized ginger*

½ cup unsweetened apple juice
2 teaspoons cornflour
Extra water to rinse

Soak the ginger for 1 hour in boiling water to remove all sugar. Chop it, and place with all the ingredients, except the cornflour, in a saucepan. Gently simmer for 20 minutes. Cool. Blend in a blender. Thicken with cornflour mixed in a little water.
  Place in a sterilized glass jar and refrigerate.
  Makes 1 cup.

Prune and date spread

1 cup prunes, pitted and chopped
½ cup dates, chopped
¾ cup unsweetened grape juice

Place all the ingredients in a saucepan. Gently simmer them for 20 minutes. Cool, and blend in a blender.
  Place in a sterilized glass jar and refrigerate.
  Makes 1 cup.

Quick tasty tomato sauce

350 g tomato paste, salt free
½ cup dates, pitted and chopped
2 medium-sized onions, chopped
1 cup water

1 clove garlic, crushed
⅓ bottle Esy Sauce* (or
  spiced vinegar)

Cook the dates, onions, water and garlic until the onions are tender. Add the tomato paste. Cool. Place into a blender and purée. Return the mixture to the saucepan and add the Esy Sauce. Gently simmer for about 30 minutes. Place in a sterilized bottle and refrigerate.
  Makes 600 ml.

---

* Esy Sauce is a commercial product obtainable at supermarkets.

Raspberry and apple sauce

1 cup fresh raspberries   *½ cup dark unsweetened grape juice*
1 cup fairly dry apple purée

Prepare and wash the raspberries. Gently simmer them in a saucepan with the other ingredients for about 1 hour.

Cool, and store in a sterilized jar in the refrigerator. Use as a topping on fruit or make a larger quantity and use as a pie filling.

Makes 2 cups.

Variation

MD   Add ½ cup dates, pitted and chopped.

RD

Raspberry spread

2 cups washed fresh raspberries
1 cup unsweetened dark grape juice

Place the ingredients in a saucepan. Gently simmer them for 30 to 60 minutes.

When the mixture is thick, cool it. Store in a sterilized jar and in the refrigerator.

Makes 1 cup.

Variation

MD   Add ½ cup dates, chopped and pitted.

RD

Sue's gravy

1 cup stock, non-fat   *1 teaspoon low-salt soy sauce*
2 tablespoons skim-milk powder   *1 tablespoon cornflour*

Mix the cornflour with a little water. Add it to the remaining ingredients in a saucepan and stir until thickened. Serve with Virginia Roast (page 56).

Makes 1½ cups.

Tomato and corn relish

2 cups ripe tomatoes, skin removed,
  chopped
¾ cup fresh corn off the cob
1 cup white vinegar
½ cup dates, chopped
¾ cup fresh or unsweetened canned
  pineapple, crushed

1 medium-sized onion, chopped
2 teaspoons curry powder
2 teaspoons mustard
1 tablespoon cornflour

Gently simmer half of the vinegar with the dates, cool, and blend. Prepare the tomatoes, pineapple, corn, and onion. Place in a saucepan with the date mixture and remaining vinegar, and simmer very gently for 1 hour. Mix together all the dry ingredients in a little water, and stir this into the mixture. Allow to thicken. Cool and place in sterilized glass jars. Store in the refrigerator.

Makes about 3 cups.

Tomato sauce

MD

2 kg ripe tomatoes, chopped
4 medium-sized onions, chopped
3 cloves garlic (extra if required)
1 cup pitted dates

1 cup natural sultanas
1 teaspoon powdered ginger
⅓ bottle Esy Sauce* (or
  spiced vinegar)

Place all the ingredients (except the Esy Sauce) in a saucepan, bring to the boil and simmer for about 1½ hours.

Put the mixture through a blender. Return it to the saucepan and add the Esy Sauce. Gently simmer it for 1½ hours. Allow it to cool slightly and place in sterilized jars or bottles. Store in the refrigerator. Delicious.

Makes about 900 ml.

---

* Esy Sauce is a commercial product obtainable at supermarkets.

Tomato zucchini gravy

1 tomato, sliced
1 cup mushrooms, chopped
3/4 zucchini, chopped
1 small onion, chopped
Pinch each garlic powder, basil,
  sage, and cayenne pepper

2 teaspoons cornflour
1/4 cup unsweetened apple juice
1 tablespoon tomato paste, salt free

Place all the ingredients, except the tomato paste and cornflour, in a
saucepan. Simmer for about 10 minutes. Thicken with cornflour mixed in
water. Add the tomato paste. Serve hot.
  Makes 1 cup.

White sauce

1 tablespoon cornflour
1 cup water, or non-fat stock
2 tablespoons skim-milk powder

Mix the cornflour with a little water. Add it to the remaining ingredients
in a saucepan. Stir constantly until the mixture thickens. If a very thick
sauce is required, add more cornflour.
  Makes 1 cup.

Stuffings

Stuffings and seasonings are tasty flavourings for many dishes.

Although meat, fish, or chicken are not permitted if you are on the Regression Diet (apart from the 100 g (3½ oz) maximum per week), you may eat small quantities of some of the stuffings cooked with them. But remember that you are permitted to eat *only the stuffing*!

If you are following the Maintenance Diet, you may eat any of the stuffings that flavour your dishes.

Apple-prune raisin stuffing

1 cup apples, peeled and chopped
¼ cup prunes, pitted and chopped
¼ cup natural raisins
2½ cups breadcrumbs (Pritikin, or
  approved bread)

⅛ cup chicken stock, fat free
¼ teaspoon paprika
¼ teaspoon cinnamon
½ cup unsweetened apple juice

Combine all the ingredients.

Apricot stuffing

½ cup onion, chopped
½ cup celery, chopped
¼ cup parsley, chopped
1 cup apples, chopped
1 cup apricots, canned in natural
  juice, drained and chopped

3 cups breadcrumbs (approved
  bread)
½ teaspoon seasoning
Pinch garlic powder

Combine all the ingredients.

Brown rice stuffing

1 cup brown rice, cooked
1 medium-sized onion, minced
½ cup celery, finely diced
1 cup mushrooms, chopped
1 cup breadcrumbs, (Pritikin or
 approved bread)

½ teaspoon seasoning
Pinch garlic powder
Small amount chicken stock,
 fat free

Combine all the ingredients and moisten with the chicken stock.

Chestnut stuffing

RD

1 cup canned chestnut purée,
 sugar free
1 cup breadcrumbs (Pritikin or
 approved bread)

1 egg white (discard yolk)
Some stock, fat free (or water)
½ teaspoon seasoning

Blend the chestnut purée and egg white, and fold in the breadcrumbs and
seasoning. Bind with the water or stock.

RD ## Parsley and thyme stuffing

1½ cups breadcrumbs (Pritikin or
  approved bread)
1 tablespoon chopped parsley

Good pinch thyme
grated rind 1 lemon
Juice 1 lemon

Combine all the ingredients and mix well.

RD ## Sage and onion stuffing

½ teaspoon dried sage
3 large onions, chopped
⅔ cup stock, non-fat, (or water)

1 cup breadcrumbs (Pritikin or
  approved bread)
1 egg white (discard yolk)

Cook the onions in water or stock for 10 to 15 minutes. Drain off the water
and fold in the breadcrumbs, sage and egg white.

Appetisers and savouries

Being on a diet doesn't mean giving up the little pleasures of life, such as party snacks or pre-dinner morsels. The appetisers and savouries in this section are very tempting, especially if they are attractively served.

Asparagus rolls

RD

9 asparagus tips, cooked and soft   *Small quantity Mayonnaise*
9 slices of approved Pritikin bread   *(page 87)*

Remove the crusts from the bread and roll out the slices thinly. Spread lightly with mayonnaise.
Place the asparagus tips on the bread slices diagonally. Roll them up tightly and chill for several hours.
Serves 9.

'Caramelled' puffed rice

MD

4 puffed rice cakes, broken up into
*   pieces to resemble popcorn*
½ cup Date Purée (page 83)

Gently spoon the purée over the rice pieces. Place on a non-stick tray and gently brown in a moderate oven, turning constantly for 10–15 minutes. Leave to cool. Store in an airtight jar.

Fruit dippers

RD

20 sultana grapes   *10 strawberries*
20 unsweetened pineapple pieces,   *10 mandarin segments*
*   drained*   *20 tooth picks*

Thread 3 pieces of any of the above fruits on to tooth picks. Arrange on a tray around Ricotta Dip (page 100).
Serves 10.

Honeydew balls and lemon sauce

MD

1 honeydew melon
2 lemons, juiced
2 tablespoons Date Purée (page 83)

2 tablespoons lemon rind
A little water

Halve the melon and make it into balls. Use the left-over melon to mix with the lemon sauce. Simmer the juice, Date Purée, rind, water and left-over melon for about 5 minutes. Cool and blend. Spoon over the chilled melon.
Serves 2.

Marinated mushrooms

RD

12 small mushrooms
2 tablespoons chicken stock, fat free

½ cup French Dressing (page 85)
1 clove garlic, crushed

Lightly brown the mushrooms in the chicken stock. Cover with the French Dressing and garlic. Marinade for several hours in the refrigerator.
    Serve on tooth picks.
    Serves 3–4.

Potato mayonnaise

*3 medium-sized potatoes, peeled
  and diced small*
½ cup Mayonnaise (page 87)

Pinch curry powder
Pinch garlic powder

Prepare the potatoes and gently simmer in water with the garlic powder until tender but *not* mushy.

Cool the potato. Coat the cubes with the mayonnaise and curry powder mixed together. Serve with tooth picks.

Serves 3–4.

Ricotta dip

*1 cup ricotta cheese, non-fat or
  1% fat (maximum)*
½ cup non-fat yoghurt, sugar free

1 tablespoon orange peel, grated
1 tablespoon orange juice

Place all the ingredients into a blender and blend. Serve the dip chilled in a glass dish to accompany your favourite salad vegetables or fruit dippers (see page 98).

Salmon cups

2 cups thick White Sauce (page 92)
220 g can pink or red salmon
12 slices approved bread
Small quantity ricotta cheese,
  1% fat (maximum) or non-fat

Small quantity of grated cheese,
  1% fat (maximum)
Parsley sprigs for garnish

Make the white sauce. Skin and remove the bones of the salmon. Wash the flesh under water to remove the brine. Gently stir the fish into the sauce.

Remove the crusts from the bread slices, roll out a little and spread very lightly with the ricotta cheese. Place each slice into muffin or small cake tins and fill with the salmon sauce.

Sprinkle with a little grated cheese and bake in a moderately hot oven for no longer than 10 to 15 minutes. Garnish with tiny sprigs of parsley. Serve warm.

Makes 12.

Variation

Curried salmon cups: Omit the cheese, add ½ teaspoon curry powder.

MD

Salmon dip

MD

220 g can pink or red salmon
1 cup ricotta cheese, non-fat or
  1% fat (maximum)

½ cup non-fat yoghurt, sugar free

Remove the skin and bones from the salmon. Wash the fish under cold water to remove the brine. Then place all the ingredients into a blender and blend. Serve chilled with salad vegetables on toasted broken pita bread to resemble potato chips.

MD   # Salmon-stuffed eggs

*5 hard-boiled eggs, halved (remove
  and discard yolks)*
220 g can pink or red salmon
*½ cup ricotta cheese, non-fat or
  1% fat (maximum)*

¼ teaspoon curry powder
Pinch garlic powder
Parsley to garnish

Remove the skin and bones from the salmon. Wash the flesh under water
to remove the brine. Place all the ingredients, except the eggs, into a
blender. Put into a forcer bag and fill the 10 egg halves.

Place the 'eggs' on to a plate of lettuce leaves. Garnish with tiny sprigs
of parsley.

RD   # Watermelon cocktail

2 cups watermelon balls
1 orange, juiced

Pour the juice of the orange over the melon balls. Cover and chill. Serve in
cocktail glasses. Garnish with fresh mint.

Serves 3–4.

102

Beverages

These hot or cold drinks have delectable flavours. There are many more beverages that can be devised, just by using a little imagination and keeping within the allowances and guidelines of the diets.

Any variety of fresh fruit may be blended with skim milk to make a milk-shake.

If possible, use fresh fruit to make juices. If you can't, many fruit juices are available in bottles or cans and are suitable for use, but always remember to read the labels carefully to make sure that the beverage is sugar free and salt free and has no artificial flavouring, colouring, or additives and preservatives.

Use caffeine-free coffee and tea substitutes or herbal teas.

If you are dining out, you could take with you a bottle of unsweetened carbonated apple juice as a gift.

Banana yoghurt drink

1 cup yoghurt, sugar free and
  non-fat
1 cup banana, sliced
¼ cup liquid skim milk

1 tablespoon Date Purée (page 83)
¼ teaspoon vanilla
Pinch nutmeg
2 ice-cubes

Combine all the ingredients in a blender and blend on high speed.
  Serves 2.

Grape juice punch

4 cups grape juice, unsweetened
1 cup fresh orange juice
2 bottles carbonated apple juice,

with no added sugar, artificial
flavourings or colourings
Ice-cubes

Combine all the liquids, and float the ice-cubes on top.
  Serves 10–12.

Hot cappuccino exchange

2 cups liquid skim milk
2 teaspoons caffeine-free coffee
  substitute

Carob powder

Place the heated skim milk and coffee substitute into a deep jug. Beat at high speed until frothy. Pour into coffee cups. Lightly sprinkle with the carob powder. Serve Hot.
  Serves 2.

Hot spiced orange

4 cups fresh orange juice (or
  unsweetened)
1 cinnamon stick

Grated nutmeg
4 extra cinnamon sticks (optional)

Heat the orange juice with the cinnamon stick. Remove cinnamon stick and pour the juice into hot glasses.
  Top with grated nutmeg. Garnish with the extra cinnamon sticks if you like.
  Serves 4.

MD # Pineapple-orange punch

3 cups unsweetened pineapple juice
3 cups fresh orange juice
2 bottles carbonated apple juice,
  with no added sugar, artificial
  flavourings or colourings

¼ cup unsweetened pineapple pieces
5 strawberries, halved
1 orange, thinly sliced in rounds
Ice-cubes

Combine all the liquids, and float the fruit and ice-cubes on top.
Serves 6–8.

MD # Prune shake

2 tablespoons cooked prunes, stoned
  and chopped
1 cup yoghurt, sugar free and
  non-fat

1 cup liquid skim milk
1 tablespoon Date Purée (optional)
  (page 83)

Place all the ingredients into a food processor and thoroughly mix. Serve
chilled.
Serves 2.

Cereals and pastries

A rich source of vitamins and minerals is found in the enormous variety of grain and cereal foods available on the market today. These foods may be eaten raw or cooked at any time of the day or night in unlimited quantities. But try to vary the types of grain you eat daily.

It is worthwhile trying to buy grains and cereals that have been organically grown. They should be free of sugar and salt. Also, buy biodynamic brown rice, make it up, and keep it in the refrigerator to use for various dishes.

You can make up your own breakfast muesli with the grains of your choice.

During the day, have an extra bowl of oatmeal if you are hungry.

To make the pastries, you can buy stoneground wholemeal flour, or grind your own.

RD # Cooked oatmeal

1 cup rolled oats, sugar free
1½ cups cold water

Mix the ingredients in a saucepan. Bring to the boil, and gently simmer until the rolled oats are cooked, but not too thick. Add more water if necessary.

Top with unprocessed bran, or grated apple, or mashed banana. Serve with a small amount of skim-milk liquid.

This is a good sedative if you have trouble sleeping.

Variations

MD Top with 8 natural sultanas, or 4 pitted dates, or 4 chopped raisins.
RD Combinations of rolled cereal grains may be used instead of rolled oats.
RD Rye flakes, barley flakes, triticale, rolled wheat, millet.

RD # Helene's muesli

3 cups rolled oats *1 cup wheat flakes*
1½ cups rice flakes *1 cup triticale flakes*
1 cup millet flakes *2 cups unprocessed bran*
1 cup barley flakes *Or other grains of your choice*

Mix all the ingredients and add 1½ cups unsweetened apple juice. Place the mixture in shallow trays at 120°C for 2 hours. Stir gently every half hour as it browns.

Cool, and place into large airtight containers.

Serve daily as required.

MD Ingredients and directions as above until removal from the oven. Then add ¾ cup natural sultanas to each tray.

Variation

This muesli can be used as a biscuit-base when placed into a blender and ground, or used as a topping on desserts as a garnish.

Oatmeal 'crumb' pastry RD

2 cups rolled oats, sugar free
6 tablespoons unsweetened apple
 juice

2 tablespoons lemon juice

Place the rolled oats in a food processor and process until they resemble crumbs. Add the juices and mix gently. To use as a base for pies, slices, and so on, press it into a foil-lined dish.

Add 6 pitted, chopped dates. MD

Savoury wholemeal pastry RD

1½ cups stoneground wholemeal SR
 flour
½ cup stoneground wholemeal
 plain flour
1 egg white (discard yolk)

1 cup liquid skim milk
Pinch grated nutmeg
Pinch garlic powder
Pinch cayenne pepper

Mix the dry ingredients, add the egg white, and mix to a pastry dough with the skim milk liquid.
   Use some of the flour on the board when rolling out the dough.

Sweet wholemeal pastry RD

As for Wholemeal Pastry, but use unsweetened grape juice or apple juice instead of skim milk.

Variation

As for Wholemeal Pastry, but add 1 tablespoon Date Purée (page 83). MD

Wholemeal pastry RD

1½–2 cups stoneground wholemeal
 SR flour
1 egg white (discard yolk)

Quantity of liquid skim milk
Extra flour for the board

Mix the ingredients together with enough of the milk to make a pastry dough. Roll out and use for savoury, vegetable or meat dishes.

Index